A History of The Western National

A History of
WESTERN NATIONAL

R. C. Anderson F.C.I.T.
&
G. G. A. Frankis M.C.I.T.

DAVID & CHARLES
Newton Abbot London North Pomfret (Vt)

British Library Cataloguing in Publication Data

Anderson, Roy Claude
   A history of Western National.
   1. Western National Omnibus Company – History
  I. Title   II. Frankis, Geoffrey
  388.3'22'065423   HE5664.7W/

ISBN 0–7153–7771–X

Library of Congress Catalog Card Number: 79-51082

Typeset by ABM Typographics, Hull
and printed in Great Britain
by Redwood Burn Limited, Trowbridge and Esher
for David & Charles (Publishers) Limited
Brunel House, Newton Abbot, Devon

Published in the United States of America
by David & Charles Inc.
North Pomfret, Vermont 05053 USA

Contents

Introduction and Acknowledgements

No history of Western National would be complete without reference to the other major operators of buses and coaches in the 'Nationals' territory, for their activities have had a direct bearing upon the development of Western National. Our aim in this book has been to trace the history and development of road passenger transport (including buses and tramways) in South West England, with particular emphasis on Western and Southern National, their constituents and their competitors.

Since the history of The Western National Omnibus Co Ltd is dealt with in full, this must inevitably contain references to developments in portions of Gloucestershire and Wiltshire, which are not strictly within the accepted definition of South-West England.

The book has been written against a background of many changes in road passenger transport industry in England and Wales and we would express our gratitude to K. H. Wellman, General Manager, Bristol Omnibus Co Ltd, and Ian Campbell, General Manager, Western National Omnibus Co Ltd for their overall help and encouragement.

While some difficulties occurred in respect of a minority of smaller independent operators the response to our enquiries was generally excellent. Many local operators were kind enough to supply details of their history and fleet, particularly M. I. Collins of Pearce and Company, Cattistock, and W. S. Baker of Hutchings and Cornelius Services Limited, South Petherton.

G. Kelly and the late H. Pitts, former employees of Western National kindly supplied several of the interesting historical photographs relating to Devon Motor Transport, Hardy-Colwills and other early operators. Particular thanks are due to Alan Watkins who allowed several of his photographs to be included. Finally, we must thank Brian Barrett who wrote the Foreword.

Special mention must be made of the *Tramways of the West of England* by P. W. Gentry and to various articles by R. C. Sambourne on local tram and bus systems in the West. The authors also read extensively many articles published over the past twenty years and express their general indebtedness to *Motor Transport, Old Motor, Bus and Coach, Modern Transport, Buses, Buses Illustrated, Tramway Review, Passenger Transport, The Railway Gazette,* and *Omnibus Magazine.*

In this book we have attempted to record within the limits available to us the story of bus and coach development in South West England from the introduction of motor vehicles until early 1979.

R. C. ANDERSON

G. FRANKIS

May 1979

R. C. Anderson, recently Operations Manager (South) of National Travel (South West) Ltd and Manager of Greenslades Tours Ltd, is currently South West Project Leader of the NBC Market Analysis Project.

G. Frankis is Senior Traffic Assistant of the Western National Omnibus Co Ltd and the authors stress that the opinions in this book are theirs and must not in any way be construed as representing the views, official or unofficial, of the National Bus Company.

Foreword

Buses, unlike trains, are not inherently romantic things, perhaps because they tend to be more commonly used and thus taken for granted. Nobody would think of reopening a closed bus route like they would a closed railway line. Here we have the root cause of the lack of glamour of the bus. A bus is a bus is a bus and very little has changed since the business began within the living memory of many people still alive today. The train, however, very much the senior partner of the bus, has evolved from steam to diesel to electric motive power and it is arguably this which gives the train its undeniable fascination.

However, be that as it may, Western National is one of the most romantic bus companies, helped no doubt by the role played by the Great Western Railway in shaping its destiny and the acquisition in later days of the most romantic of all coach operations, Royal Blue. This history, written by two people who have been intimately involved in the development of Western National, brings to life the excitement of the early days, the more mature period of consolidation and the less happy times of contraction in the face of changing market requirements.

History does not stop with the writing of their books and the future of Western National is still of importance, not only to its staff but to its users, for without it their means of basic mobility would be no more. Journeys to work, to school, to shops, to visit friends and relations, just could not take place otherwise for very many people living in the South West.

As is so often the case, the future is in doubt for many and various reasons, but let us hope that those who have a say in shaping the future of Western National can learn from the experience of the past as encapsulated in this book, and that people elsewhere can gain from sharing the achievements and tribulations recorded within its pages.

B. M. M. Barrett

Regional Planning and Development Officer, Midlands and West Region National Bus Company

LYNTON & LYNMOUTH
(via Barnstaple).
*Four-horse Coaches in connection
with Fast Trains run as follows:*

			A.M.	
LYNTON	....	.... dep.	8 0	....
Barnstaple	....	.... ,,	1113	....
			P.M.	
Exeter (Queen Street)	....	arr.	1230	....
Plymouth (North Road)	....	,,	2 19	....
Plymouth (Friary)	....	,,	2 31	....
Salisbury	....	.... ,,	2 49	....
Southampton	....	.... ,,	4 20	....
Portsmouth	....	.... ,,	4 44	....
WATERLOO	....	.... ,,	4 40	....

			A.M.	
WATERLOO	....	.... dep.	9 15	....
Portsmouth	....	.... ,,	9 25	....
Southampton	....	.... ,,	9 45	....
Salisbury	....	.... ,,	1130	....
Plymouth (Friary)	....	.... ,,	1130	....
Plymouth (North Road)	....	,,	1143	....
			P.M.	
Exeter (Queen Street)	....	,,	1 45	....
Barnstaple	....	.... ,,	3 35	....
LYNTON	....	.... arr.	6 30	....

1 General Background

Apart from the formation of a few horse-drawn tramway and bus systems in certain urban areas towards the end of the nineteenth century, the development of bus services in the West Country as in most other parts of the country really began with the opening of the present century. In the almost 80 years since then the bus industry has seen dramatic changes in its fortunes and structure, as it has become predominant, particularly as branch and cross country railways were closed, and then subservient to the challenge of private motoring. The story of bus services and operators in the South West can conveniently be divided into six main periods, which form the theme of this chapter.

1. The years 1900-14

This was a period of experiment with a new, capricious and slightly humorous toy—the internal combustion engine. Motor bus services were a strange and sporadic innovation by a handful of visionary pioneers; the dyed-in-the-wool transport man stuck to horses, electric trams, or of course the railways. It may come as a surprise to many to learn that it was nevertheless the railways and in particular the road motor department of the GWR, under the guiding hand of F. C. A. Coventry, which can claim the major credit for pioneering early motor bus services in the West in the days before World War I. When, in 1903, the GWR's two chain-driven Milnes Daimlers bumped their way over very inadequate roads from Helston station to the Lizard, they were doing more than save the GWR £85,000 on the construction of a light railway, they were ushering in a new

11

era in the history of transport. The GWR venture was a great success and its rapid development over the next 25 years is recounted in Chapter 2. Their example prompted Mr Wolsey of Thomas Tilling to experiment with a motor bus on one of the London horse bus routes and also fired the imagination of Sidney Garcke of the British Electric Traction group; both groups were later to play leading parts in the development of provincial bus services both generally and in the West of England.

Meanwhile, on the other side of England in Essex, Thomas Clarkson was expanding his business manufacturing steam propelled buses and in 1906 formed the Chelmsford Steam Car Co Ltd. This was the infant which three years later became the National Steam Car Co, the predecessor of Western National, Southern National and Eastern National. Thus, before the present century was ten years old, the principal actors had already been introduced.

Meanwhile, in those Edwardian days, while motor and steam buses chugged around rather precariously, it was the electric tram that held the centre of the stage where urban transport was concerned.

The tramways of the South-West are summarised below:

Town	Year Horse Trams Introduced	Year Electric Trams Introduced
Exeter	1882	1905
Plymouth Stonehouse & Devonport Tramways	1872	1901
Plymouth Devonport & District Tramways	1884/5 (Steam)	1901
Plymouth Corporation Tramways	1893	1899
Taunton	None	1901
Torquay	None	1907

The ownership, fortunes, idiosyncracies and later replacement by buses, of these various tram systems will be traced under the relevant bus companies in the chapters that follow.

A preview of those early years would not be complete without mention of Thomas Elliott's Royal Blue services at Bournemouth, which were to have such an impact on long distance coach operation in the years to come. Royal Blue commenced its four-in-hand stage coach service in 1880 and remained loyal to horse traction until 1913, when it purchased two motor char-a-bancs.

2. The years 1919-27

World War I gave a great impetus to the development and improvement of the internal combustion engine. Moreover,

driving experience for thousands of young whom on return to civilian life seized the nvest their gratuities in the motor bus. In the ee years there was a rapid and unrestricted services all over the country. There were no ctions and anyone could acquire a bus and rever, whenever and at whatever fares he the period of the pirate bus, of racing on the gers and cut-throat competition in fares, but e period when the present pattern of bus he West was becoming established.

of vehicles used have been the subject of lications and those interested are referred to ns of The Omnibus Society and the PSV Circle, who have produced historical fleet lists. Tram-cars are listed in *Tramways of the West of England* by P. W. Gentry and Colin Shears of Exeter has an excellent collection of old buses in North Devon, which are displayed to the public from time to time.

The Devon General Omnibus & Touring Co Ltd was founded in 1919 and within three years had amalagamated with the Torquay Tramways Co Ltd (a subsidiary of the National Electric Construction Co). As the National Electric Construction Co was later acquired by the British Electric Traction Co (BET), the formation and development of Devon General marked the establishment of BET interest in buses in the West, although the Taunton Electric Traction Co Ltd and the Devonport & District Tramways Co Ltd both started life as BET subsidiaries.

It is interesting to note that 1919 also saw the beginnings of what was to become the Tilling interest in the West. In that year the traditional 'National' stronghold in Essex was expanded and a foothold was established in Stroud, Gloucestershire. On 13 February 1920 the company was reconstituted as the National Omnibus & Transport Co and from its original base in Stroud, the company expanded south and west, absorbing small operators and opening up new routes. Meanwhile, further west, that great pioneer busman, Commander Hare, founded the Devon Motor Transport at Okehampton in 1920, with buses staffed by ex-service personnel. His network spread rapidly throughout West Devon. Then he transferred his company's head-quarters to Plymouth and formed a subsidiary, Cornwall Motor Transport, which exploited bus services in East Cornwall.

Commander Hare is probably the only bus personality in the West whose name has lived on from the early days. From the passengers' point of view, the local man, whether he is the proprietor of a private concern or the local super-intendant of a large company, personifies the bus company. Head offices appear somewhat remote and the fact that the larger companies were subsidiaries of holding groups meant that the entrepreneur was not a feature of the bus business. It is interesting that several proprietors of small concerns are women: Miss Gunn of Safeway Services, South Pether-ton, is a well known character in the Yeovil area. Large companies have found it prudent to decentralise management as far as possible so that the local organisation retains personal contacts and is sensitive to local events and passenger trends, while head office management exercises overall control and carries out national policies. This is the basic difference from purely local ownership but, on the other side of the coin, the national operator is expected to maintain standards and facilities which do not generally pertain to the small operator.

In the field of long distance coach services Royal Blue, under the direction of Thomas Elliott's two energetic sons, had motorised its fleet of char-a-bancs and in 1919 commenced a weekend experimental service between Bournemouth and London. This met with instant success and was gradually built up to a daily service during the 1920s. From Bristol, Greyhound Motors Ltd commenced its Bristol-London coach service in 1925. Also in 1925 both the National Omnibus & Transport Co Ltd and Royal Blue were two of the constituent companies in the formation of London Coastal Coaches, the first association of long distance service operators.

By 1927, the road passenger transport industry had reached a turning point. The two large holding groups, BET and Tilling, which had more or less stood on the sidelines in the West, were poised ready to move in and assume more direct control; the days of unfettered competition had reached a critical point and it was obvious that the government was going to impose some form of control in the interests of road safety and the general stabilization of an industry which had grown far faster than anyone anticipated. Finally, the vehicles themselves had developed and improved with the introduction of pneumatic tyres and other refinements, to the point where the term 'luxury coach' could rightly be employed, and long distance services were poised for a rapid and dramatic expansion. During the following

15

four years the whole character and ownership of bus and coach services in the West thus changed.

The British Electric Traction Co was formed in 1896 as a holding company to promote tramway companies and electric lighting undertakings. Realising the potentialities of motor buses, in 1905 the group formed British Automobile Traction to set up bus services on a similar basis. Meanwhile, Thomas Tilling Ltd had started a horse bus undertaking in London in 1851 and in 1904 it too realised the significance of the new motor vehicle and introduced petrol electric buses on London routes. By 1913 Tilling and the London General Omnibus Co were in conflict and an agreement of that year limited the number of Tilling buses in London to 150. Tillings therefore sought outlets for expansion outside London, and its interests coincided with those of the British Automobile Traction group, with the result that in 1928 Tilling and British Automobile Traction Ltd was formed. Meanwhile, each of the two groups had separately obtained a controlling interest in certain bus undertakings, so that the pattern of ownership which emerged was either Tilling, or BET, or joint Tilling and British Automobile Traction.

3. The years 1927-31

This four-year period was one of change and grouping, rather like the railway grouping of 1923. The first significant move was the acquisition in November 1927 by the National Omnibus & Transport Co of Devon Motor Transport and Cornwall Motor Transport. Commander Hare joined the National Board, but so venturesome a pioneer could not long be chained to group policies and the following year he left to found Jersey Motor Transport and subsequently went to Africa, where he was responsible for the inception of a dozen or more new bus undertakings. Professionalism and restrictive nationalism have little room for such men.

In 1928 radical changes were taking place in the railway operated bus services, and doubt was expressed as to whether they had the necessary legal powers to engage in road services. Such powers were obtained in 1928, but the railways decided, rightly or wrongly, to exercise them by investment in BET, Tilling, T & BAT and National groups, rather than by direct operation themselves. Negotiations between the chairman of the National Omnibus & Transport Co and the Great Western Railway ended in agreement in December 1928 to merge the railway bus services and the National bus services, splitting the latter into the territories of the respective railway companies, i.e. Western National (GWR), Southern National (Southern Railway), Eastern National (LNER) and Midland National (LMS). The new, separate companies, still under National Omnibus & Transport Co control but with railway participation in the shareholdings, were registered in February, 1929. At the same time Northern National Omnibus Co Ltd was also registered as a non-trading company, to prevent anyone else using the name. In the event it has never functioned; moreover Midland National did not operate as a separate entity and remained part of the Eastern National system. From 1 January 1929 the GWR transferred all its buses and services in the West to Western National, with the exception of one service in the Weymouth Area which passed to Southern National in 1934. The registered offices of the three National companies continued at 206 Brompton Road, London, formerly the office of the National Omnibus & Transport Co, and three managers were delegated to look after Eastern, Southern and Western National at Chelmsford, Yeovil and Plymouth respectively.

The final moves took place in May 1931 when the National Omnibus & Transport Co Ltd was acquired by Thomas Tilling Ltd by increasing share capital and borrowing money in the open market. At the same time the National

Electric Construction Co was acquired by BET, and by the end of 1931 the two major holding companies were firmly established owners of the main bus undertakings in the West.

The greater flexibility and smaller capital costs of the motor bus made itself felt and the years 1927–1931 saw the replacement of tramway systems by buses at Camborne/Redruth and Exeter.

Significant changes also took place in the sphere of legislation and the relationship of the Government to road passenger transport. It had become increasingly apparent that the rapid growth of motor bus services and of road traffic in general called for some new form of control and in 1928 a Royal Commission on Transport was set up. During the 1920s, control was supposedly exercised by the local authority licensing system in those areas where hackney carriage regulations were in force. Operators wishing to provide public transport in these areas had to obtain a licence-plate from the appropriate local authority and fix it to their vehicles. Such a licence could be granted or refused as the council saw fit and to it could be attached whatever conditions relating to equipment and any other matters the council deemed appropriate. The system was designed for horse-drawn transport within a limited radius and when the wider ranging motor bus and long distance coach came along, the position became quite absurd. Each authority acted in isolation and sometimes in contradiction to its neighbouring authority, and the mounting of all the licence-plates of each authority on every vehicle became an impossible task, particularly in the case of long distance services when the backs of vehicles could be covered with plates of all shapes and sizes! In practice, one bought a bus and started to operate where one chose; it was dangerous and not in the public interest in the matter of regular and reliable service. The 1928 Royal Commission recommended in respect of road passenger transport:

(a) The Licensing of vehicles, to ensure they came up to a proper standard of repair and maintenance;

(b) The Licensing of drivers and conductors to ensure adequate standards of behaviour on the roads;

(c) The Licensing of services, including timetables and faretables, to obviate unfair competition and ensure that a reliable standard of service is provided for the travelling public.

All these recommendations were embodied in the Road Traffic Act, which became effective on 1 August 1930, and which also provided for the setting up of traffic areas with Traffic Commissioners to administer licensing provisions. The Western Traffic Area administered from Bristol covers the area which today forms Western National territory.

The physical strife between rival operators on the roads was now transferred to legal strife in the Traffic Commissioners' courts and the road service licence became a vital document, without which a bus service could not be provided. Generally, the industry welcomed the 1930 Act and it is noteworthy that the main provisions relating to the licensing of services, buses, drivers and conductors are still applicable. However, the requirements of the Act in respect of vehicle design and the relation between seating capacity and manning, inhibited one-man operation on larger vehicles, and put an end to some promising one-man developments notably in Plymouth and Southampton; it has taken over 30 years to rectify the position.

There was a rapid expansion in the long distance coach field during 1928/9, sparked off by the formation of London Coastal Coaches three years earlier and by the desire to stake a claim before the recommendations of the Royal Commission on Transport passed into law.

4. 1931-39 The years of consolidation

By its very nature, the 1930 Road Traffic Act was followed by a period of consolidation. It imposed new terms of reference on providers of public transport and the whole industry took on a more technical nature, requiring greater expertise. The early 1930s were the years of the great legal battles, when the detail of the Act, the interpretations and precedents had to be fought out in the courts. Though conducted on a more civilised basis, the struggle between operators was if anything sharper than in the days before the Act, for if one's case was lost in the traffic court, the opportunity was gone for ever. Many of the smaller operators, unable or unwilling to be fettered by the demands of the new legislation, were glad of the opportunity to sell their businesses to the large companies. The latter also were in a better position to buy up small concerns, since the subsequent obtaining of the licences gave an undisputed right to the route, whereas before the Act any new operator could have started running in competition. From the mergers of the 1927-31 period and the stabilising influence of the 1930 Act, arose the large territorial companies. By agreement with neighbouring associated companies, each large operator established itself in a defined area or territory, which the adjacent operators undertook not to breach. Cross boundary services were (and still are) the subject of joint agreements and joint operation. The territorial companies cannot be described as monopoly operators, since small independent and private operators continue to provide services within the defined territories and both the Traffic Commissioners and the local authorities have considerable powers in relation to facilities provided.

The first large organisational change in this period was the formation of Associated Motorways in 1934, to organise and control long distance express services of the constituent companies. This was quite a revolutionary development—

a partnership of limited liability companies, with the express road service licences held in the name of the group and not of the individual members, and revenue allocated in proportion to the percentage of mileage operated within the pool by each member company. The original six partners in Associated Motorways were Black & White Motorways Ltd, Red & White Services Ltd, Elliott Bros (Bournemouth) Ltd (proprietors of Royal Blue services), Birmingham & Midland Motor Omnibus Co Ltd, Greyhound Motor Services Ltd and United Counties Omnibus Co Ltd. The scheme, mainly based on routes radiating from Cheltenham to all parts of England and Wales, expanded and prospered, several more member companies being added as services developed.

Another major development took place in 1935, when Elliott Bros sold the Royal Blue Express coach business to Thomas Tilling Ltd on behalf of its subsidiaries Western and Southern National. The development of Associated Motorways and Royal Blue is described in *A History of Royal Blue Express Services* published by David & Charles, though now out of print.

The trams at Torquay ceased in 1934 and in Plymouth the Corporation had embarked on a programme of tram replacement in 1931; by 1938 only one tram route remained. The tram, so full of promise during the first decade of the century, had proved a short-lived form of transport, largely because of its lack of flexibility in an increasing pattern of traffic and its higher capital cost than the motor bus. The unfortunate provisions of the Tramways Act of 1870, permitting the acquisition of undertakings by local authorities after a specific number of years at very low valuation, also militated against the development of tramways.

In 1938 the Devon General and the National companies finally signed a territorial agreement defining their respective spheres of operation.

5. The years of World War II, 1939-45

The War years were inevitably an interlude in the progress of the bus industry, with austerity and improvisation as the guiding principles. Fuel rationing was severe, especially for private cars, so that reduced bus services had to bear the burden of increased passenger loadings. The standing passenger regulations were temporarily relaxed under wartime emergency powers and it was no uncommon sight to see roads virtually empty of all traffic except buses bursting at the seams with passengers. The strain on vehicles was considerable, especially as new buses and spare parts were very difficult to obtain, all available factories having been converted to armament and military vehicle production. From 1943 a thin trickle of utility buses, on a very austere pattern with wooden seats, began to be available. Meanwhile, to employ the slender resources of passenger vehicles to the full, loans and exchanges between companies and corporation undertakings were extensively made. Many vehicles were earmarked for military purposes, some were adapted for air raid ambulances and the whole position was further worsened by the havoc wrought by enemy air action. In Plymouth, both the Corporation and Western National suffered severe losses by air raids.

To combat the growing fuel shortage, gas propulsion was tried as an alternative to petrol and diesel oil, not the inflated gas bags on the roofs of vehicles, as was done in World War I but producer-gas, generated in anthracite burners incorporated as trailers behind the buses. Nevertheless, the growing national shortage of fuel as the war progressed could not entirely be offset and in October 1942 the Government ordered the cessation of all express coach services. For the remaining three years of the war only essential basic stage services and works/military contracts were operated.

The Ministry of Transport also took steps to simplify the

licensing procedure and in each traffic area the Traffic Commissioners were replaced by one Regional Transport Commissioner. Road service licences were replaced by permits which ran for an indefinite period, and the traffic courts procedure was also suspended—there was no need for them, as the Regional Transport Commissioner decided what services were essential in the national interests and there could be no question of competing applications to tap new markets.

The war had one curious side effect in that it prolonged the life of such tramways as still existed, since the electric tram was not dependent upon imported fuels. The last remaining tram route in Plymouth was retained 'for the duration' even though the town centre section had to be abandoned in 1941 because of bombing.

But even during the war, the slowly evolving pattern of the bus industry continued and two significant events must be recorded. The first was the agreement in 1942 between Tillings and BET to end the joint control of subsidiaries through the T & BAT organisation and to share out the companies involved between the two holding concerns. The second event, important because it was to typify the co-ordination of post war years, was the establishment of the Plymouth Joint Services scheme between Plymouth Corporation and Western National in 1942. This joint arrangement was largely precipitated by the war, principally the serious losses incurred by both parties in the savage air raids on Plymouth which made it essential to pool vehicle resources, and by the dispersal of population from the inner city area to the surrounding rural districts. Under the Joint Services scheme, all bus services within a defined area around Plymouth were pooled and receipts and mileage divided in an agreed proportion between both parties; all fare restrictions on Western National services entering the city were swept away, and vehicles were freely interchanged

23

as needs arose. The scheme, which has served as a pattern for joint operations around other towns and cities, has continued to flourish, enabling Corporation vehicles to go outside the confines of the city boundaries and enabling Western National to share in the remunerative town traffic.

6. The Post World War II period, 1946 to date

The 30 or so years since World War II can themselves be subdivided into two periods, the first five years of expansion and then a quarter century of contraction:

(i) 1946–50: *the years of recovery, re-equipment and expansion.* The end of the war found bus companies in a run-down condition; fleet replacements were urgently required, vehicles commandeered by the military were returned in poor condition, damaged depots needed repair or rebuilding. With the return of normal civilian life, there was an unprecedented demand for bus services, both for men returning from the forces to industry and for recreational purposes after the austerity of the war years. In the spring of 1946, express coach services began to be resumed step by step, as vehicles and staff could be found. Meanwhile, stage carriage services rapidly reached pre-war level and then built up steadily until, by 1950, the bus industry was at its peak, with more buses in operation, more routes and more places served than ever before or since. These were good years in many respects; the chronic inflation of costs had not started and bus fares were still at pre-war level. The roads and villages of England had not yet disappeared under a blanket of moving metal and after the alarms of war, life for a few precious years had a quiet and dream-like quality. People enjoyed themselves soberly, with little television and without transistors, and travelled almost entirely by train, bus or coach.

A background theme to the post-war story of the bus industry, is its developing relationship with the State.

Whether governments should run businesses, or whether they should confine themselves to the art of wise government, is a matter for future historians to judge, when catch phrases like 'free enterprise' and 'socialism' will have lost their emotional connotations. Nevertheless, governments all over the world do engage in industries and particularly in transport; the advantages of overall planning and of community interest as opposed to profit are attractive and obvious—the disadvantages of commercial issues becoming entangled in conflicting political considerations and the inability of large government agencies to make rapid decisions or quick adaptations, are not so obvious. However, whatever the merits or demerits, Thomas Tilling Ltd decided to sell the whole of its very large bus interests to the Government in 1947 and were followed by the Red & White Group in 1950. By the Transport Act of 1947 they passed into the control of the British Transport Commission together with the railway shareholdings in the BET companies. Thus, in one important move, the State became owners of more than half of the country's road passenger transport industry. The 1947 Act also contained powers for setting up Area Schemes in which the entire transport system would be compulsorily nationalised, but the scheme promulgated for the West was so bitterly opposed by all the local authorities and remaining independent operators that it was finally abandoned when the post-war Labour Government went out of office. Fortunately, the former Tilling concerns retained their company basis and were enjoined to continue as separate commercial entities, with local control, the only difference being that the share capital was government owned.

In 1947 Devon General and Exeter Corporation concluded a Joint Services agreement covering Exeter on similar lines to the Plymouth scheme of 1942.

(ii) 1951–75: *the years of recession and adaptation to falling*

25

traffic. When petrol rationing ended in 1950 everyone breathed a sigh of relief at the passing of yet another wartime restriction. But few foresaw that over the years this return to normal plus the increasing standard of living which gradually placed private motoring within the reach of most families would practically strangle public road transport, both by loss of passengers and by traffic blockage within town centres. Despite increasing population and the centralisation of schools which has resulted in a great increase in scholars' travel, bus undertakings have experienced a steady passenger decline of 3–4 per cent per annum since 1953. This pattern of declining traffic, coupled with the spiral of increasing costs has meant that bus undertakings have had to resort to fare increases almost annually since the 1950s. A full account of fare structures and the development of fare scales can be found in *Fare Structures in British Road Passenger Transport* 1920-72 by G. Frankis, available in the Chartered Institute of Transport library. Services in rural areas, where the impact of private transport has been greater than in towns, have been progressively reduced or abandoned and the bus map of the late 1970s looks very different from that of 1950. In addition, many of the small independent operators in the West have either gone out of business or drastically reduced the number of services operated. The major bus companies while judiciously pruning their services, tended to take the view that the public would prefer to keep facilities and pay more by way of increased fares, and until 1971 directed the main weight of their economies towards the single manning of vehicles, dispensing with conductors. Since the war, the regulations governing the permitted maximum length of vehicles have been changed progressively from 27ft to 39ft and single deckers can now accommodate as many passengers as the pre-war double decker. One-man double deck operation is therefore only necessary on heavily loaded city or inter-urban routes.

Another important factor in the changing pattern of transport during the past 20 years has been the closure of most of the railway branch lines in the West and their replacement by substitute bus services. Because of its predominantly non-industrial nature and generally sparse population, the West has incurred more rail closures than any other part of England and the process which had been going on since 1950, was greatly accelerated after the publication of the Beeching Report in 1963. In many cases, in agreeing a rail closure, the Minister of Transport ordered the provision of replacement bus services. The general comment can be made that, in practically every case, these substitute bus facilities proved totally uneconomic and worsened the burden of unremunerative operations which rested so heavily on bus undertakings. Railway closures, for some reason, seem to raise quite disproportionate passions and political issues are drawn into the subject, but many villages and towns have managed to exist without railways and those fortunate enough to possess them have no claim to rail service (or replacement bus service) as of right.

The Transport Act of 1953 did little to alter the existing relationship between bus companies and the government; in the main it divorced the government's road transport interests from its railway interest, so that the profitability of the former could be seen and not swallowed up in the deficits of the latter.

In 1953 a further move was also made in the consolidation of road transport interests in the West, when BET obtained control of Greenslades Tours Ltd of Exeter, a major tours operator within the area of Devon General (already a BET company). Under the impetus of the new ownership, Greenslades rapidly expanded its tour business in the ensuing six years, buying up local operators until it had virtually a monopoly of the tour business in the coastal resorts on each side of Exeter.

The Transport Act of 1962 placed the shareholdings of the government-owned bus undertakings under the newly formed Transport Holding Company. It also established the Area Transport Users' Consultative Committees, which have played a leading role in subsequent railway closures.

Further moves in the changing pattern of bus ownership came about in 1968 and 1969. During 1968 there was much discussion both inside and outside parliament of the controversial clauses of the government's new Transport Bill and in the midst of all this it was announced that BET had agreed to sell its bus interests in Great Britain to the Transport Holding Company. An enabling Act was passed, authorising the Transport Holding Company to increase its borrowing powers to carry out this major purchase. The Transport Bill finally became the Transport Act 1968, which among other things replaced the Transport Holding Company with the National Bus Company (NBC) from 1 January 1969. The wider repercussions of the Transport Act, its effect on drivers' hours, the powers granted to local authorities to make grants towards the maintenance of unremunerative bus services and the future outlook for the road passenger transport industry, will be examined in the final chapter of this book.

The National Bus Company was conceived as a means of offering the public and local authorities a progressive, dependable bus system. The structure of the company gives bus systems local control supported by central policy-making. As an organisation it employs around 65,000 people and owns approximately 18,000 buses and coaches. The NBC is a holding company with some 40 subsidiary companies and groups and each subsidiary is required by statute to be separately accountable as far as finances are concerned.

To ensure that continuing consultation and co-operation between British Rail and NBC subsidiaries exists, standing joint committees of responsible officials meet at frequent intervals to discuss and agree matters of common concern.

One of the obvious outward signs has been the corporate identity of the vehicles, buildings and staff uniforms featuring the double N symbol. Buses are now in common liveries of green or red and coaches in white livery.

Many operators from outside South West England have contributed to the pattern of road passenger transport in the area. Concurrently with the development of the bus companies described in this book, services have developed from as far afield as Scotland and East Anglia, conveying many thousands of holidaymakers to and from the western counties. In addition the South West is the venue for an extensive range of day tours, extended coach touring holidays and private hire. Coaches operate into the area in connection with tours to the mainland of Europe through Plymouth and Weymouth, where buses and coaches feed the Britanny Ferries or Sealink shipping services to France and the Channel Islands.

Since the formation of the National Bus Company, several tidying up moves have already taken place in the West. For many years, the old distinction between 'Southern National' and 'Western National' as reflecting the respective share holdings of Southern Railway and Great Western Railway, had ceased to have any significance, and towards the end of 1969 it was decided that retrospectively from 1 January 1969, the Southern National Omnibus Co Ltd should become dormant, all its operations being merged into the Western National Omnibus Co Ltd.

From 1 January 1970 the Trowbridge and Chippenham depots of Western National were transferred to the Bristol Omnibus Co Ltd, terminating the Western National enclave which had existed within the Bristol area since 1919. At the same date, the registered offices of Greenslades Tours Ltd and the Devon General Omnibus & Touring Co Ltd (and its subsidiaries Bute Court Garages Ltd and Court Garages (Torquay) Ltd) were transferred to Western National headquarters in Exeter. The Court Garages tours business became part of the Greenslades organisation on 2 May 1971 and subsequently the Bute Court business was wound up and the property sold.

In 1972 the National Bus Company placed Greenslades Tours and its other coaching subsidiaries under the control of its then Central Activities group to form the nucleus of the National Travel organisation. A further change took place in 1978 when several Greenslades depots including the Torquay operations were transferred to Western National.

From 1 April 1970, taking advantage of the powers granted to local authorities under the Transport Act to dispose of their transport undertakings, the City of Exeter sold its bus system to the National Bus Company which placed it under the control of the Devon General Omnibus & Touring Co Ltd.

Another major development affecting public transport was the passing of the Local Government Act of 1972, which came into operation on 1 April 1974 in England and Wales and 1 April 1975 in Scotland. Among its many wide-reaching provisions, which reorganised the entire set-up of local authorities, this Act placed a much wider responsibility for transport on County Councils and Metropolitan Counties. They became responsible for the co-ordination of all forms of transport within their areas (including private cars) and were enjoined to submit 'Transportation Policies and Programmes' annually to the secretary of state for the environment. At last the way seemed open for the overall control and co-ordination of transport and traffic, including traffic management schemes in city centres for placing the emphasis on public rather than private transport. County engineers or county surveyors set up departments within their organisations presided over by a transport manager (or equivalent title) to discharge the counties' obligations under the Act. The Act left the running of municipally-owned bus fleets with the second-tier authorities (the district or city councils) and did not transfer them to the county councils, which became co-ordinators and policy-makers rather than actual operators. Obviously these provisions entailed the spending of a great deal of public money in the establishment of transport and traffic patterns directed towards the well-being of the community at large. The situation may be summarised by quoting part of Section 203 of the Local Government Act 1972 which gives county councils the duty 'to provide a co-ordinated and efficient system of passenger transport'. The Transport Act 1978 adds to this duty the requirement for county councils 'to develop policies which will promote the provision of a co-ordinated and efficient system of public passenger transport to meet the County's needs'. Currently Western National is working in conjunction with county councils in carrying out a major survey of all its bus services as part of the National Bus Company's Market Analysis Project.

Already the county authorities in the South West have achieved several useful objectives in the exercise of their new transport powers. Devon County has gone ahead with its plan for creating a pedestrian precinct in High Street, Exeter with lanes for buses only and this has done much to restore the ancient quiet and dignity of this old cathedral city. The County has also sponsored a network of summer services on Dartmoor and Exmoor to assist walkers and to help reduce heavy private car traffic. Cornwall County Council has revived a series of market-bus services around Truro, based on one vehicle serving a different group of villages each day (Monday to Friday).

So far as the Western National Omnibus Company is concerned, since 1974 there have been useful negotiations

31

with county councils which have resulted in the restoration of bus services over certain sections of routes which had been abandoned in previous years. These items are dealt with in greater detail in Chapter 3. The timetabling of school contract journeys where there is sufficient accommodation for members of the public in addition to scholars, or the timetabling of empty running before and after working school contracts, has also been encouraged by county councils, and has resulted in a number of additional services or journeys. The only drawback with such operations is that, unless specifically subsidised by the county councils, they cannot be operated during school vacations.

A major feature of Western National's operations was its service network operated under the fleet name Royal Blue. This name is still carried by the coaches but the express services are now part of the National Travel organisation which is described in Chapter 5.

Before concluding this chapter, two general matters should be mentioned. First, working conditions for employees in the tramway and early bus industries at the turn of the century were hard, and with the emergence of trade unions, it is not surprising that there was a demand for union representation in these industries. After sporadic strikes and unrest, a big step took place in March 1919 with the conclusion of an agreement relating to hours and conditions of work between the National Transport Workers Federation and representatives of the associated municipal transport undertakings and the Tramways and Light Railways Association. In September of the same year, a National Joint Industrial Council for the tramway industry was set up, with equal representation of employers and employees. Over the years, this form of national negotiating machinery has been extended and it now covers, separately, staffs employed in provincial bus companies (i.e. NBC subsidiaries and certain private operators) and municipal undertakings. In the case

(*top*) LSWR buses in Chagford Square circa 1905. (*Western National*); (*above*) one of the original GWR buses operated on the Lizard peninsula. (*Western National*); (*below*) GWR bus at Penzance railway station before departure for Lands End. (*Western National*)

(*top*) DMT Bristol at Tamerton Foliot. (*Collection of H Pitts*); (*above*) a Hardy-Colwill Leyland at Ilfracombe on the Westward Ho! service, 1926. (*G Kelly*); (*below*) Southern General vehicle (former 'HB Buses') at Broadhempston.

of the majority of the small private operators, the union negotiating procedures do not as yet apply and their staffs are paid under the 'fair wages' clause of the Road Traffic Act 1960, although a recent decision of the Arbitration, Conciliation and Advisory Service may well see substantial changes in this situation in the not too distant future.

Second, safety regulations within the industry can be traced back to the Board of Trade inspections of tramways, to the notorious 'Red Flag Act' of 1865 (which required an attendant with a red flag to walk in front of all mechanically propelled road vehicles) and to various subsequent Locomotive and Motor Car Acts, culminating in the Road Traffic Act of 1930. Since that date, public service vehicles, the routes they cover, their drivers and conductors, have been subject to the control of the Traffic Commissioners for the appropriate Area. This, together with various general road traffic regulations, the high standards set by the major bus operators and the professional skills of their staffs, have made the British bus or coach one of the safest forms of transport in the world.

2 The Predecessors of the Western and Southern National, and Early Days in Plymouth

Compared with most other large bus companies, Western National was formed at a comparatively late date (1929) and consisted of a fusion of several separate pioneer undertakings, each with a distinct and interesting story of its own. It is a fairly complex period and in tracing the formation and development of these component undertakings up to 1929 the evolution of passenger transport in Plymouth itself is an essential part of the story, since the intricacies of Plymouth Corporation Transport and its forerunners cannot easily be separated from those leading to the formation of Western National.

Among the predecessors of Western National may be claimed some surviving stage coaches, because in the West Country the stage coach was not entirely superseded by railway developments in the nineteenth century. In West Dorset, for example, there were three horse coach services in 1905 between Lyme Regis and Bridport, Bridport and Crewkerne, and Charmouth and Axminster. On the first of these, which took two hours for the journey (present Western National bus, 36 min), the fare was 4s (20p) single, 7s (35p) return, compared with the present bus fare of 54p single. Coach travel was apparently for the gentry and humbler folk had to be content with the carriers cart or their own two legs. The Ilfracombe-Bude four in hand stage was still working at this time—though there is no comparable through bus or coach service between these towns at the present day! But most colourful of all were the *Lorna Doone*, *Katerfelto* and *Red Rover* four horse stages, which, with the help of an additional two horses at Porlock and Countisbury (and the assistance of able-bodied passengers who dismounted and walked!) clawed their way regularly over the mountainous road from Minehead to Lynmouth in three hours during the years when Porlock Hill and Countisbury Hill were beyond the capabilities of the emergent motor bus. These famous stage coaches did not cease until 1922 when they were ultimately superseded by a motor bus service.

The Road Passenger Services of the railway companies

The railways' interest in motorbus services and, indeed, the story of motor buses generally in the West, begins in a most unexpected quarter with the tiny narrow gauge Lynton & Barnstaple Railway, which opened in 1898. Passengers from Ilfracombe to Lynton had to be conveyed by horse coach to Blackmoor Gate station and in 1903 the chairman, Sir George Newnes, tried to mitigate the unpopularity of this procedure by establishing the Ilfracombe Motor Co to operate two motor coaches via Berrydown, to avoid the long climb out of Combe Martin. The coaches were open 16hp Milnes-Daimler machines with solid tyres, no windscreens or doors and passengers sitting four abreast in five ascending tiers—and two beside the driver. Those in the back row had to climb a six-rung ladder to their seats! The experiment lasted three months, as the local magistrates, determined to prevent this undesirable motor traffic in their area, inflicted a very heavy fine when one of the buses travelled at just over 8 mph. Sir George in disgust, sold his two motor buses to an undertaking which was destined to have far better fortunes. This was the road motor department of the Great Western Railway, set up in 1903 by the foresight and energy of F. C. A. Coventry, who realised that certain sparsely inhabited regions of the West could never justify branch or light railways and saw in the emerging motor bus a suitable substitute. When one recalls the inflexibility and iron will of traditional railwaymen at this time, when railways were at their peak, the vision and purpose of these pioneers in the road motor department can be seen in true perspective.

On 17 August 1903 the two Milnes-Daimlers were put into operation between Helston station and the Lizard— a strange and outlandish spot for the birth of provincial motor bus transport! They were soon supplemented by additional vehicles of similar type but of a weight in excess of three tons, which until the repeal of the Red Flag Act in 1904, would have necessitated a man walking in front with a red flag! To circumvent this, pieces of equipment were removed from the vehicles to bring the weight down for official classification purposes and were subsequently restored. From the start, the railways' venture into road transport was a success and the Lizard service was followed on 31 October 1903 by one from Penzance (Newlyn) to Marazion and on 3 April 1904 by the Penzance—Lands End route. From 1 May 1904 the GPO used the Helston—Lizard route for the conveyance of mails, but towards the end of the year the service had to be suspended because of the refusal of the local authority to re-metal the road or allow it to be rolled, coupled with a fire at Helston depot resulting in the loss of two vehicles. However, by mid 1905, the difficulties with the council had been resolved, the depot re-opened and the service resumed. Other early bus routes started by the GWR in West Cornwall were:

Penzance—St Just, 16 May 1904 (with double deck vehicles); this replaced a service started the previous year by the West Penwith Motor Co Ltd which failed;
Redruth—Portreath, 29 July 1907;
St Austell—Bugle, 3 August 1908.

Developments further east in the Plymouth area were not far behind and on 2 May 1904 the first GWR bus service in Devon was introduced between Modbury and Yealmpton (connecting with the Yealmpton—Plymouth railway line). Sir Tristram Eve and a local company also ran a competing bus over this route under the title of South Hams Motor Carriers Ltd; they were bought out by the GWR in 1905 and this must rank as one of the first takeovers in the motor bus industry. The service was subsequently extended from Yealmpton into Plymouth. On 1 June 1904 the twice daily horse-drawn conveyance between Saltash and Callington was superseded by GWR buses at a return fare of 2s. (10p). Pre World War I developments in the Plymouth area were completed in September 1904 by the opening of a service from Plymouth to Crownhill and Roborough. By 1913 the GWR fleet in this area comprised six Milnes-Daimlers, three garaged at Plymouth and three at Yealmpton.

Further east a depot was opened at Weymouth in 1905 with a service between Radipole Spa and Wyke Regis. This service was withdrawn in 1909 when rail motor units were introduced on the parallel railway but three years later (22 July 1912) the London & South Western Railway, in conjunction with the GWR resumed road operation with Milnes-Daimler and Dennis vehicles. This joint LSWR/GWR service continued to a later date than any other of the railways' bus routes and was not taken over by Southern National until 1 January 1934.

Depots were opened in 1905 at Stroud and Winchcombe, the latter being closed in 1906 when the Winchcombe—Cheltenham railway opened. On 9 April 1906 a Moreton-hampstead—Chagford motor bus service was inaugurated. All GWR road services were primarily designed as feeders to various railheads or as alternatives to the construction of uneconomic branch or light railways. Subsidies for passenger services, so much in the news since the Transport Act of 1968, are no new thing, for in 1903 the GWR was paying more than £1,000 a year in subsidies to thirteen operators of horse conveyances transporting passengers to railheads. The introduction of its own motor bus services enabled these payments to be saved. In 1905 a central repair depot was established at Slough.

The pioneer efforts of the London & South Western Railway must not be overlooked for in 1905, in an obvious effort to beat the GWR to Moretonhampstead and Chagford it purchased two Clarkson steam buses and inaugurated an Exeter Queen Street (now Central)—Whiddon Down—Chagford service. For four years this route was maintained by steamers and anyone who knows the hills involved can appreciate the stalwart efforts of these early steam buses. In 1909 they were replaced by Thornycroft petrol-engined vehicles. The steam bus generally was superseded, not because of any inherent mechanical defect, but because of the high cost of repairs and replacements; indeed during the first ten years of the century their smoothness of running and hill-climbing abilities were superior to those of the petrol engine.

In those days petrol was 4d. (1½p) per gallon but the most expensive single items on the early buses were the solid tyres, which cost £200 per set and worked out at 1½p per mile. This expense almost caused the abandonment of the entire project. Running like an uncertain thread throughout the period of GWR bus operation, was a lack of specific statutory powers to operate road services, a position not clarified until the late 1920s. Nevertheless, despite these uncertainties and the difficulties in obtaining suitable types of vehicles during 1905/6 (the Milnes-Daimler chassis was by then in great demand and Durkopp, Wolseley and Clarkson vehicles were not wholly satisfactory) the GWR bus fleet showed a steady expansion:

Dec 1904: 34 vehicles (when the GWR fleet was greater than London's omnibus fleet!)

June 1905: 56 vehicles

Dec 1905: 72 vehicles

Dec 1906: 80 vehicles (67 being Milnes-Daimlers)

Jan 1908: 113 vehicles (106 being Milnes-Daimlers, of which 14 were double deckers).

The first buses were open to the weather but on 12 October 1903 the first fully enclosed bus body was brought into service: it had one acetylene interior lamp and five headlights!

The Lizard service was met at strategic points along the route by donkey carts for the transfer of mail to and from outlying villages. Driving one of these buses presented problems quite unknown to present day drivers; brakes were neither effective nor reliable, the wheel brake consisting of a wooden shoe acting directly on to the surface of the rear solid tyres, while on hills the conductor walked beside the bus with a scotch in his hand, ready to place it in position if the vehicle came to a halt. Some buses had sprags which dug into the road surface as a brake, and others had brakes which might burst into flames if used on long downhill stretches. Road surfaces were at best waterbound macadam, being extremely slippery in wet weather and correspondingly dusty in dry weather; open bodied vehicles had to be fitted with special dust shields. The driver had to perform a juggling act to keep the vehicle going, manipulating three separate speed change levers and replenishing two glass oil bottles on the dashboard from a long spouted can, while at his own discretion, pumping oil from these bottles into the engine. It was no unusual thing for a driver to stop on the road and re-time his engine. Breakdowns were frequent and many a driver spent the night with his vehicle after hiring horses to take the passengers home, while the conductor walked back to the depot to report. Certain vehicles were adapted as 'luggage omnibuses' with slightly cheaper fares; they carried virtually everything either inside or on the roof —linoleum, crates of fish, bicycles and even roped pigs and calves.

Vehicles were usually garaged at the appropriate railway stations, each depot being in charge of a leading driver but conductors were under the control of the station masters and cash was paid in to the booking office as clerical staff were non-existent before World War I. Railway type tickets were issued at first, but later, bell punch machines were used. There were even books of tickets at 12½ per cent discount, foreshadowing the present weekly or season tickets. Staff uniform consisted of leather cap, jerkin, waistcoat, breeches, gaiters and greatcoat.

The GW railway colours of chocolate and cream were mainly used for livery but there were variations, some buses having red bonnets. In retrospect one cannot but salute the determination and confidence of the GWR management in its perseverance with so quixotic a form of transport and the adaptability and devotion of staff in keeping the vehicles on the road. Had conditions and outlooks been as today, the whole project would probably have been abandoned after a 'feasibility study' or the staff would have been seeking substantial incentives to persuade them to work the vehicles.

World War I petrol shortages resulted in the reduction of services and the closing of certain depots (e.g. Plymouth in 1916); during this period some of the older vehicles were converted to goods lorries and parcel vans. Several buses were operated on coal-gas, which was contained in gas bags roped to the top of the vehicle. In high winds these gas bags occasionally broke loose and were pursued across country by the bus crew. On one occasion a bus carrying mail broke down and the crew persuaded a passing hearse to take the letters on to the railway station. Women were employed as conductors during the war and also as drivers on parcel vans.

After the war, the internal combustion engine had proved its worth and was no longer a tentative, capricious, experiment. For the ten years from 1919 there was a rapid expansion of motor bus operation and the GWR kept in the forefront of developments, opening up new routes throughout its territory. In 1921, the statutory right of the GWR to engage in motorbus operation was called into question by rival interests but after discussion it was decided not to issue a restraining injunction to challenge this right in view of the undoubted public value of the facilities being provided. In 1925, however, the GWR's rights were disputed through the London and Provincial Omnibus Owner's Association and as a result agreements were concluded with Devon Motor Transport and Cornwall Motor Transport, allocating routes between the three undertakings and eliminating wasteful competition. In particular certain GWR activities were discontinued in favour of Cornwall Motor Transport.

The Plymouth—Roborough service was not resumed after World War I, but the Modbury route was developed and became a through Plymouth—Kingsbridge—Dartmouth operation. The railhead at Kingsbridge became the focal point for a number of services radiating into the peninsular to the south, in particular to Salcombe and Hope; services were also inaugurated from Plymouth to Bigbury-on-Sea, and Noss Mayo. There was competition on the Plymouth—Yealmpton—Newton Ferrers section from Devon Motor Transport until the 1925 agreement. In Devon, further GWR developments took place in the Paignton/Totnes area in 1905 with a frequent service between these two towns (164 journeys per week by 1929), a Paignton—Greenway route and latterly, in 1929, Paignton local services purchased from Messrs Ashcroft and Kent. Further west in Cornwall the GWR developed a Truro—St Austell service in 1920 together with journeys from Grampound to Tregoney and

Portscatho, bringing public transport to the villages of the
Roseland peninsula for the first time. Here again on the
Truro—St Austell route, the GWR interests clashed with
Cornwall Motor Transport but were sorted out by agree-
ment in 1924. The final position of the GWR in Cornwall
was:

(a) Services from St Austell, including the Truro main
     road and Truro—Portscatho;
(b) Services from Helston, including a connecting link
     with Penzance;
(c) Services from Penzance to the West;
(d) A long distance connecting route Plymouth—
     Falmouth and Helston, commenced in 1921.

Since there was a parallel main line railway, the GWR
did not develop bus services along the trunk road from
Penzance through Camborne and Redruth to Truro, which
left the way open for Cornwall Motor Transport.

To the east, in Somerset, Gloucester and Wiltshire, the
GWR bus network was less extensive, although it started the
Bridgwater—Minehead route and also had a small group of
services based on Frome and Stroud. In 1924 a depot was
opened at Marlborough and a service was inaugurated
between Swindon and Wantage.

During the period 1919–1924 the entire pre-war fleet,
with the exception of some Maudslays acquired in 1913, was
replaced by more modern vehicles mainly of AEC manufacture. These new vehicles were in green livery, the colour
generally adopted for GWR passenger vehicles for several
years, after which the original chocolate and cream was
reintroduced. No further double deckers were purchased and
the last one saw service at Weymouth. For use on lightly-
loaded rural services, a number of one-man operated
Burford 18 seaters and ten light, 14 seater Chevrolets were

acquired. The Burfords and Chevrolets were the first GWR vehicles with pneumatic tyres and no subsequent buses had solid tyres. They were followed by a series of Thornycroft 18–20 seaters, mostly one-man operated.

The growth of the GWR involvement in bus operation during the 1920s can be illustrated by the following figures of the number of services worked:

1920	44	routes
1923	54	,,
1924	71	,,
1925	97	,,
1926	114	,,
1927	148	,,
1928	154	,,

During their last three years of operation (1927–9) the GWR commenced services at Weston-Super-Mare, Portishead, Westbury and Newbury together with long distance links, e.g. Swindon—Burford—Banbury, and Oxford—Burford—Cheltenham. The latter, started in 1928, did not pass into the control of Bristol Tramways and Carriage Co Ltd until 1932, three years after the main transfer of railway bus services. During these last three years, 200 new Maudslay and Guy 32 seaters were placed in service.

Throughout 25 years of bus operation the GWR continued to show the same energy and enterprise. Local tours tentatively commenced before the war, were resumed in 1920 and developed throughout the western counties, while in 1927 'land cruises' were commenced, offering 6–13 day extended tours of Exmoor, Dartmoor, the Wye Valley, North Wales, etc. The land cruises were operated with three 15 seat Thornycroft parlour coaches, the height of luxury at the time.

In August 1928 the railways at last obtained comprehensive road powers, and acting from a position of legal strength, decided to give up direct operation in favour of large scale investment in major provincial bus companies. It was in many respects a sad decision and marked the end of a great tradition of service and a great pioneering effort. At the end, the GWR was working 168 services with 300 vehicles, throughout its territory. Nevertheless, a large proportion of its road operations was concentrated on Devon and Cornwall, and when, in January 1929, the Western National Omnibus Co Ltd was formed, it was on the basis of an amalgamation of GWR services with those of the National Omnibus and Transport Co Ltd rather than a railway investment in an existing bus company. The railway employees engaged in bus operation were given the option of transfer to the newly formed company, retaining their railway rates and privileges and were termed 'loaned staff'; the last one, Edgar Biscombe, retired from Western National in July 1974 from Dartmouth depot.

The end of the railway story came on 17 August 1953 when a special plaque was unveiled in the station wall at Helston. It consisted of a bronze inscription mounted on a granite block, with the wording 'This tablet commemorates the opening of the first railway motor omnibus service which was run by the Great Western Railway from Helston to the Lizard 17 August 1903. Erected 17 August 1953'. Now Helston station has itself closed and only ghosts of the once Great Western Railway remain. Yet as events turned out it was not quite the end, for in 1978, to mark the 75th anniversary of The Lizard service, once again a bus painted in chocolate and cream livery bearing the initials GWR—this time a Leyland Atlantean—could be seen operating the service between Helston and the Lizard, as a tribute to one of Western National's forebears.

The National Omnibus & Transport Co Ltd

Compared with the GWR and with the Devon and Cornwall Motor Transport and Hardy-Colwills whose stories follow, the National's was not a great pioneering effort. Its policy was one of supplying finance and expertise to buy up and co-ordinate existing operators, in which it was successful, for by 1930 it had emerged as the predominant bus company in the West.

The National Steam Car Co had been going through a period of crisis in the year following the end of World War I. Many vehicles had gone to France during the conflict and not returned; in addition, the steam bus had been outstripped by those with the internal combustion engine. The company was in debt for large sums of money and the time had come either to give up, or completely revise the company's pursuits and policies. The latter course was adopted and two important decisions were taken, first, by an agreement in 1919 with the Underground Group (parent Company of the London General Omnibus Company) the National undertook to withdraw from London entirely and to devote the capital obtained thereby to provincial expansion and the last steam bus worked on Service 12 Dulwich—Shepherd's Bush on 19 November 1919. The second decision was to transfer to petrol engined vehicles and the first three Dennis buses were licensed in Essex in June 1919. The natural corollary was a change in the name of the Company from the National Steam Car Co to National Omnibus & Transport Co which occurred on 13 February 1920; the head office was established at 206 Brompton Road, London.

It would not be true to say that the National did not pioneer the opening of any bus routes. Stroud depot, opened in October 1919 was a true pioneer exercise in developing new services and this was followed in 1920 by the opening of depots at Taunton and shortly after at Bridgwater, allowing the operation of the trunk route

Taunton—Bridgwater—Burnham-on-Sea, one of the principal Western National services in Somerset to the present day. The original National 'office' at Bridgwater was a wild west affair—two planks on boxes on a site at East Quay with the vehicles 'garaged' in a blacksmith's yard. Later they were stationed in a yard at the Steam Packet Inn and subsequently under cover on the premises of Real, Medland and Willis Ltd. 1920 also saw the first acquisition by the National Co when the Nailsworth—Stroud—Gloucester service of F. J. Arnold was purchased. At the beginning of 1921 the National fleet in Bridgwater consisted of two open top double deckers for the Taunton—Burnham route, one single decker which worked to Weston-Super-Mare and Glastonbury, and one char-a-banc, all on solid tyres. In these early days, the running time was one hour Taunton—Bridgwater and 50 min Bridgwater—Burnham and it was no unusual thing for 100 passengers to be crowded on to the open toppers, many of them standing upstairs; on approaching the railway bridge over Bristol Road someone would shout and everyone would duck to avoid decapitation!

In 1921 National also opened a new depot at Yeovil and in May of that year important developments took place in the provision of transport within Taunton town. The Taunton trams were one of the smallest and shortest-lived systems in England, although registered in 1900 under a magnificent title 'The Taunton and West Somerset Electric Railways and Tramways Co Ltd'. The original plan envisaged Taunton as the centre of a vast tramway system radiating into the countryside on reserved tracks and through fields, rather like the Belgian tramways; places as far out as Wellington, Wiveliscombe and Curry Rivel were to have been served. The company was a subsidiary of the British Electric Traction group. Construction commenced in 1901 and resulted in one length of street tramway (single track with passing loops) from Taunton Station to East Reach

(Hamilton Road), a distance of little over one mile. Service commenced in August 1901 with six open top double deck Brush cars seating 50 passengers each and the smallness of the tramway was compensated for by the elegant livery of dark lake lined in gold, and cream lined in red. Normally a 10 min service with four cars was operated but this was augmented to a 6 min frequency with five cars at peak hours and on Saturdays. By 1903 the company realised it would never achieve its original aims and modified its title to Taunton Electric Traction Co Ltd. In 1905 disaster overtook the tramway with the subsidence of the track foundations at several points. Service had to be suspended while the entire track was relaid and on resumption the six double deckers were replaced by six new Brush single deckers. In 1909 the track was extended northward from the station to Rowbarton (Salisbury Street) giving a total route length of $1\frac{2}{3}$ miles. The trams continued uneventfully until after World War I but crisis overtook the undertaking in 1921. Vehicles and track badly needed renovation and the town council demanded increased charges for current; in addition, the National had appeared on the scene with motor bus competition. After offering the system to the Corporation for £7,000 and being refused, the tramway company decided there was no future in continuing—they refused to meet the increased power charges and on 28 May 1921 power was cut off and the tramway closed. From then on National had a free hand in developing town services in Taunton which have built up over the years to the present five routes.

The opening by National of a depot at Trowbridge in the latter part of 1921 marked the end of its activities as innovators; from then on its spectacular expansion was achieved through the rapid assimilation of existing operators. From this small bridgehead of three depots, Bridgwater, Taunton and Yeovil (Stroud and Trowbridge can be regarded as enclaves of operation within territory already staked out by the Bristol Company), National was to expand in some eight years to become the major operator of road passenger services in the South West.

The first move was southward to Weymouth, where apart from the railway operated road service between Radipole and Wyke Regis, bus operation was commenced during World War I by J. Turner on a three mile route from the Esplanade to Overcombe on the Preston Road. Mr Turner was an enterprising individual who, having retired as an engine driver on the GWR turned his hand to this new venture; he lived on to the ripe age of 95, and died in 1955. However, it was in 1920 that bus services began to play a full part in the life of Weymouth, with the formation of the Weymouth Motor Co, its first route being Weymouth—Bournemouth. Other operators quickly followed within the next year or two, Mr Rugg with a Weymouth—Chickerell—Langton Herring route and Jeanes Bros (White Star Bus Services) between Weymouth, Preston and Osmington. Several coach tour operators also came into being in 1921 and 1922, including Greyhound Coaches (Mr R. G. W. Austin) who, in 1925 as Victory Motors (Weymouth) Ltd, operated long distance express services to Portsmouth and London (via Salisbury). In 1923 the National made a tentative appearance in Weymouth with a summer only operation but later, in 1925, with the acquisition of Weymouth Motor Co Ltd and Road Motors Ltd it established itself as the predominant operator and opened a depot in the town.

National lost no time in expanding southwards into Portland Island by the purchase of the Isle of Portland Motor Bus Co Ltd in 1926 and the bus business of Messrs Smith and Hoare in 1927. Neither was the original depot at Stroud neglected and in 1927 the bus services of Major H. Napier Rowlett, Rodborough Common, Stroud were acquired. But it was in the latter half of 1927 that the principal movements began to take place; first, by the

(*top*) One of the original Grey Torpedo Cars on the Dartmouth tour, 1913. (*Western National*); (*above*) Torquay Tramways AEC on the Newton Abbot-Dawlish service 1921. (*Western National*); (*below*) Cornish Buses Limited ADC with Mumford body. (*W Mumford Ltd*)

(*above*) Western National Bristol ECW single deck bus, 1934. (*Western National*); (*below*) Western National garage at Plymouth, the morning after the disastrous air raid of 1941. (*Western National*)

purchase in July of Hardy Central Garage Co Ltd (trading as Hardy Colwills) of Barnstaple and the lesser business of Sam Edwards and Co of Bude, the National in one move established itself as the major operator throughout North Devon and North Cornwall. Only four months later, in November 1927, the acquisition of Devon Motor Transport Co Ltd (and its subsidiary Cornwall Motor Transport Co Ltd) placed National in control of large areas of South Devon and Cornwall although the company had in fact staked a claim in Plymouth a few months earlier by starting a Plymouth—Tavistock service. Hardy Colwills and Devon Motor Transport were such large and interesting businesses that they merit separate histories and are dealt with later in this Chapter. A further minor acquisition in 1927 was that of J. Kershaw of North Petherton, Somerset (near Bridgwater). During these very busy years National does not appear to have developed its Yeovil depot with the same energy apparent elsewhere and until recently three major independent operators remained, Hutchings and Cornelius of South Petherton, H. R. & V. Gunn also of South Petherton and R. E. Wake of Sparkford, which will be dealt with in chapter 6.

1928 saw negotiations with the GWR for the final major development in the pattern of bus services in the West. Meanwhile National established itself in the tours field in Cornwall by acquiring Trelawney Tours Ltd of Penzance and Hockings Tours of Newquay. Expansion in Dorset continued with the establishment of a depot at Bridport through the purchase of Kirtcher and Dunham and of Butler Bros (Bridport) Ltd. The fleet livery from 1919 to 1929 was green and white, with 'National' in large gilded capital letters on the centre side panels.

The end of the National story came in January 1929, when the railways agreed to invest in two new companies, The Western National Omnibus Co Ltd and The Southern

National Omnibus Co Ltd whose headquarters continued at Brompton Rd London with area managers at Yeovil and Plymouth. The areas associated with the GWR became 'Western National' and those associated with the Southern Railway became Southern National. Roughly this means that in 1929 Western National was formed from the previous GWR road services, together with the ex Devon and Cornwall Motor Transport interest, plus the original National depots at Stroud, Trowbridge, Bridgwater and Taunton; Southern National was formed from the Hardy Colwills interests plus the original National depots at Yeovil, Portland, Weymouth and Bridport. As at January 1929 the National fleet in the West consisted of 225 vehicles and the GWR fleet 115.

Before leaving National the seasonal long-distance coach services started in the last two years of their existence, London—Weymouth in 1927 and London—Ilfracombe, Bude, Penzance and Newquay in 1928 should be noted.

The *General Rules and Regulations for Drivers and Conductors* was issued by the National Omnibus & Transport Co Ltd on 1 August 1927—a comprehensive publication which could well serve as a model for present-day operators, apart from one or two oddities such as 'The wearing of clogs by Drivers on service is not permitted' and 'When a bus is about to pass under a low railway bridge or low overhanging trees, the driver must bring his vehicle to a standstill and passengers are to be duly and audibly warned (sufficient to cover a case of deafness of any passenger) . . .'

The list of National depots in 1927 (ie after the acquisition of Hardy Colwills but before the purchase of DMT and CMT) is interesting:

Barnstaple	Bishops Stortford
Bedford	Bridgwater
Bideford	Bude

Chelmsford
Clacton-on-Sea
Colchester
Grays
Hatfield
Huntingdon
Ilfracombe
Luton
Lynmouth
Minehead
Newquay
Portland
Romford

St. Ives (Hunts)
Shepherds Bush
Stony Stratford
Stroud
Taunton
Trowbridge
Waltham Abbey
Ware
Watford
Westward Ho!
Weymouth
Yeovil

A green supplement issued in 1929 contains 'Special Instructions to Great Western Men' and lists the following additional depots, which gives an excellent indication of the extent and coverage of the ex GWR operations:

Aberystwyth
Birkenhead
Birmingham
*Bovey
Bristol
*Callington
*Camborne
Cheltenham
Chipping Norton
Corwen
Cradley
Dolgelley
Exeter
*Falmouth
*Helston
*Kingsbridge

*Liskeard
*Moretonhampstead
Newbury
*Okehampton
Old Hill
Oswestry
Paddington
*Paignton
*Penzance
*Plymouth
Pwllheli
*Redruth
*St Austell
*Saltash
Shrewsbury
Slough

*Stroud	Wantage Road
Swindon	*Westbury
*Tavistock	Weston-super-Mare
*Torpoint	†Weymouth
*Trowbridge	Worcester
*Truro	Wrexham

*Denotes depots absorbed into the new Western National Company

†Transferred to Southern National in 1934.

Hardy Colwills

North Devon and North Cornwall were served by the London & South Western Railway (later the Southern Railway), which did not share the enterprise of the GWR in commencing road passenger services, and bus development followed somewhat different lines from the remainder of Devon and Cornwall. During the 1890s a few horse bus services were in operation as feeders to railheads or to fill gaps in the rail network, eg Bideford—Clovelly—Hartland—Bude, Bude—Boscastle—Tintagel—Camelford, Ilfracombe—Combe Martin—Lynton, Barnstaple—Lynton. The two leading personalities at this time were Mr R. Dymond who, with his sons, was working regular services from Bideford to Westward Ho! and Appledore, and Mr Sam Colwill of Ilfracombe who, starting with horse drawn carriages in the 1880s, was by 1900 operating horse buses to a number of villages around Ilfracombe. They were known as 'Sam Colwills Greys', since from the start his entire stable consisted of grey horses! Whereas Mr Colwill went from strength to strength, Mr Dymond's activities were sadly inhibited from 1901 by the opening of the Bideford—Westward Ho! railway (a BET subsidiary), extended to Appledore in 1908.

The activities of Sir George Newnes have already been mentioned in this chapter but another and more permanent memorial to his enterprise is the Lynton—Lynmouth Cliff Railway, opened in 1890 and still working without modification to this day. It is the longest and steepest of all British funiculars and since it is worked by water only, seems likely to go on indefinitely. Apart for Sir George's abortive bus attempts in 1903, there were few experiments with motor buses in North Devon before World War I, although Mr Dymond ran an open top double decker between Bideford and Westward Ho! briefly in 1909, followed by a similar unsuccessful attempt by the Westward Ho! railway with vehicles borrowed from an associated BET company. In these pre-war years the one and only 'acceptable' excursion from Ilfracombe was of course by Sam Colwill's elegant 'four in hand' to Lynton and back.

In 1916 Mr Dymond experimented with motor buses with more success and by 1920 under the fleet name of Royal Motors, was running his Westward Ho! and Appledore services on a regular frequency. The parallel railway had been requisitioned in 1917 and its locomotives shipped off to France; it was never reopened, the rolling stock being sold in 1921 and the track in 1928. Mr Dymond also had a contract for the Bideford—Clovelly—Hartland mail service, which conveyed passengers—an early post bus in effect, similar to the systems which have developed so successfully in Germany, Switzerland and Austria.

Unfortunately the other pioneer Sam Colwill died in 1919 and in February 1920 a new company Colwills (Ilfracombe) Ltd was formed to take over from his widow; £3,600 was paid for the business, including the office at 107 High Street and a garage at Marlborough Road. The directors of the new Company were Capt G. C. Shiers, Claude Crosland Taylor and Henry Hill Coleridge and among other subscribers were George Crosland Taylor and Winthrop J. C. Taylor. The Crosland Taylors were none other than the pioneers of bus operation in Cheshire and North Wales, who built up the great Crosville company, which now has more than 1,000 vehicles. Colwills was thus a far flung Crosville subsidiary and under the enterprise and energy of these men motor bus services in North Devon expanded at a phenomenal rate. By 1924 33 services were in operation based on branches at Ilfracombe, Lynton, Barnstaple, Combe Martin, Bideford, Bude, Woolacombe, Newquay and Lee. The routes bore a remarkable resemblance to those of the later Southern National's North Devon and North Cornwall area (now Western National), except that Colwills also ran a daily Newquay—Truro service. The extent of integration with the parent Crosville company is indicated by the fact that nearly all the Colwills vehicles had Chester registrations (FM) and were in sequence with Crosville deliveries of the same period.

By 1924 the Crosland Taylors had decided that a subsidiary so far from their main base at Chester was a difficult proposition, and in July 1924 the Colwills business was sold to Hardy Central Garage Co Ltd of Minehead, who already had services based on Minehead, Watchet, Williton, Bridgwater and Lynmouth. The selling price of £28,340 is an indication of how much the business had been built up from its inception in 1920. With a network of 40 services stretching from Bridgwater in the east to Truro in the west (some 150 miles) this must rank as one of the most extensive of all independent operators. The headquarters were established at Barnstaple. To preserve continuity and goodwill, the fleet name of the new company was made 'Hardy Colwills' on a red and white livery. The new owners attempted to establish a footing at Tavistock in the heart of Devon Motor Transport territory. This brought about a sharp retaliation from DMT which started services from Bideford to Westward Ho! and Barnstaple. Within a month, mutual agreement was reached on operating territories and the two firms lived in harmony, with Hardy Colwills terminating at Yelverton, only nine miles north of Plymouth.

Hardy Colwills had a comprehensive parcels service, accepting goods up to 150lbs in weight (the present limit is 42lb). Perambulators and pedal cycles were of course carried and half fares for children only applied up to age of 10, although this was later raised to 12 and then the more usual 14.

The business of R. Dymond and Sons of Bideford was acquired by Hardy Colwills and in 1926 started a new service between Barnstaple and Lynton in direct competition with the Lynton & Barnstaple narrow gauge railway. There can be little doubt that this bus service was one of the main factors leading to the closure of the railway in 1935, for in this mountainous terrain the bus was able to run into villages which were impracticable for the railway.

It was this large and flourishing business which came into the hands of National in July 1927, overnight doubling its territory.

Devon Motor Transport Co Ltd and Cornwall Motor Transport Co Ltd

No company illustrates better than DMT and CMT the spirit of adventure and enterprise which was the keynote of the motorbus industry immediately following World War I. After retiring from the Royal Navy, Lieut Commander T. Hare, in concert with a group of army and naval officers, decided to exploit the civilian possibilities of the internal combustion engine which had developed so rapidly under wartime conditions. They purchased four ex army Maudslay lorries and based themselves at Okehampton in December 1919, with the original idea of transporting produce from outlying districts in the town. It quickly became apparent that people needed transport as much as goods and the vehicles were rapidly adapted with wooden seats in the front portion and a goods section at the rear. After a rather shaky start it was decided that passenger transport was more profitable than goods, and two AECs with 20 seat bodies by the Plymouth firm of Mumfords were purchased and regular bus services were inaugurated from Okehampton to Tavistock, Launceston and Hatherleigh, as well as to Exeter on certain days of the week. Commander Hare then decided to seek advice from the Bristol Tramways & Carriage Co Ltd which by 1920 was well established in motorbus operation. He returned with four Bristol 26 seater buses and the latest know how on the development and working of bus services. From then on his firm never looked back and experienced a meteoric expansion that was to make it in three years the largest operator in Devon and Cornwall.

In a letter written in 1965 Commander Hare modestly described his achievements: 'All my activities have been in the way of starting something for nothing'. Yet what a wealth of philosophy lies behind this short summary of a life's work and how greatly it contrasts with these modern days when the prevalent attitude is all too often to 'get something for nothing'. Commander Hare was one of those rare souls, perenially young, who could only find happiness in pioneering and breaking new ground. In less than ten years, he worked up his three West Country enterprises into thriving and successful businesses and then sold out to those who enjoyed administration more than adventure. But this was only the end of the first phase of his varied life in transport, for he then went off to Jersey, Malta, Cairo, Nairobi, Mombasa and Uganda, in each of which he started bus companies in the years preceding World War II. No sooner did hostilities commence than he went back to the Royal Navy for a second spell, leaving his chief assistant to hold the fort in Africa. After the war he returned to Africa to break still more new ground and bus services were started in Nyasaland, Bulawayo, Awelo, Umtali and Salisbury. Eventually these passed into the hands of the Red & White and British Electric Traction groups. Finally, in the late 1950s Commander Hare took over Windsorian Motor Coach Services Ltd. He lived quietly in retirement in a remote part of Dorset until his death in 1971. In the letter mentioned above, he went on to say:

> I was persuaded to get all this in the shape of a book and was prevailed upon to engage . . . a Ghost Writer . . . but the result was too fanciful for my liking and I did not go on with it.

Hats off to a great character, who is still remembered annually in Devon when the Devon & Cornwall Motor Transport Association meets.

Okehampton was too small a centre for DMT and its first move was to obtain a footing in Plymouth by the operation of an Okehampton—Tavistock—Plymouth service. The head office was transferred to Plymouth and by 1923 daily services were in operation from Plymouth to Yealmpton and Ermington (co-ordinated with the GWR between Plymouth and Yealmpton); Tamerton Foliot; and Ivybridge The original routes at Okehampton were retained and further development took place based on Tavistock, Launceston, Liskeard and Callington. Competition was experienced between Plymouth and Crownhill from an operator calling his buses 'Sanfairyann' but apart from this DMT had virtually a free hand in developing its territory.

In these early days it was nothing for a passenger to find a farm animal or a side of bacon as his seat companion, while on one occasion a pack of hounds and a huntsman were conveyed. One veteran driver recalls that he was once instructed to stop at a certain point and 'pick up two kids'— they turned out to be just that—young goats!

Meanwhile back in 1921 in Cornwall a similar attempt to open up bus services was being made by a retired colonel, an army captain and two others, under the name of 'Cornwall Enterprise Motors'. With three open top double deckers a daily service was inaugurated between Truro and Perranporth, followed very shortly by a Truro—Falmouth facility. In August 1921 the company secured a contract to convey employees to a factory at Newquay and the opportunity was taken during layover to operate a Newquay—Truro service. In October 1923, due to financial difficulties, Cornwall Enterprise Motors sold out to Commander Hare, who founded Cornwall Motor Transport as a sister company to his Devon enterprise. As in Devon, Commander Hare lost no time in expanding his Cornish interests; with a central depot at Truro, temporary garages were established at Bodmin, Constantine, Falmouth, Hayle, Helston, Indian Queens and St Austell. In 1924 an amicable agreement was reached with the GWR regulating the operation of services between Truro and St Austell. In March 1923, looking further afield, Commander Hare established yet another branch in Jersey as Jersey Motor Transport Co.

Meanwhile the Plymouth area was being developed further with the introduction of services to Totnes, Cornwood, Dousland, and Wembury, together with a feeder service from Devonport to Crownhill, while in 1924 the business of A. C. Turner's Tours, Plymouth, was acquired. At this time a 15min frequency was operating between Plymouth and Crownhill, and a frequent though irregular service between Plymouth and Plympton; DMT had firmly established itself as the major operator in the City, apart from Corporation facilities within the City boundary.

Neither was the area of Cornwall across the Tamar from Plymouth neglected; there was then no road bridge over the Tamar below Gunnislake, the only connection between Plymouth and East Cornwall being by Brunel's famous railway bridge or by the Torpoint and Saltash ferries. Nevertheless the Harris Bus Co Ltd had commenced a Torpoint—Antony service during World War I and immediately after the war there were various char-a-banc and toast rack vehicles to take Plymouth residents from Torpoint ferry to the popular beaches of East Cornwall. In 1925 DMT decided to open up this area and established a Torpoint—

Looe—Polperro service, linking at Looe with its Liskeard—Looe service.

By 1925 the two companies had 90 vehicles in service in a distinctive olive green and white livery. They employed almost entirely ex-service men and no effort was spared to ensure a happy ship. A welfare club was formed, with representatives elected by secret ballot from each depot; the representatives met Commander Hare and the general managers of the two companies each month. During 1925 when financial difficulties were encountered as a result of severe competition, the staff voluntarily agreed to a temporary reduction of pay; this cut was not only restored subsequently but staff were also offered shares in the company at a guaranteed 5 per cent interest.

In order to improve the finances of the company in 1926, outlying services in the Exeter, Honiton and Newton Abbot areas were sold off to Devon General Omnibus & Touring Co Ltd and the money obtained was used to develop routes in the Plymouth area and buy out some of the most troublesome competition. During 1926/7 new routes were opened up to Eggbuckland, Meavy, Shaugh Prior, Newton Ferrers and Buckfast (Dart Bridge); the frequency on the Totnes road was also stepped up and some journeys diverted via Avonwick. Competitors acquired during this period were Goad Bros Ltd, Plympton (Plympton—Plymouth service under the fleet name Ensign), R. H. Baker's 'Rex Charabanc Tours', Pioneer Saloon Bus Service of A. Facey (Plymouth—Tamerton Foliot) and the infamous Sanfairyann bus on the Tavistock road. At this time (1927) Torpoint also became a fully fledged depot with new services thence to Liskeard and Saltash and additional local services to Downderry and Seaton.

By 1927 the Company was operating 140 vehicles, mainly of Albion, Bristol and Thornycroft makes. In September 1927 passenger services were discontinued on the Camborne—Redruth tramway largely as a result of increasing competition from CMT's buses. Camborne/Redruth was the only town in Cornwall to have a tram system, the first effort having been made in 1898 when the order for a tramway with a branch to Portreath was rejected because of the narrow roads and strong objection from the GWR. However, undeterred by this setback, the Urban Electric Supply Co Ltd made another effort in 1900 and was successful. Construction went ahead immediately on a three mile single track with passing loops from Camborne (Commercial Square) to Redruth (West End) and services started in October 1902. The next year the company was unique in introducing a freight service under contract to East Pool and Agar Ltd conveying tin ore from East Pool Mine to the smelting works at Tolvaddon ($1\frac{1}{2}$ miles). For this purpose spur tracks were laid of $\frac{1}{4}$ mile from Pool to East Pool Mine and $\frac{2}{3}$ mile from Carn Brea depot to Tolvaddon works. The fleet consisted of six open top double-deck cars seating 50 passengers, and two single-deckers; livery was dark green lined in gold, with white lower panels lined in black. For mineral traffic there were two open electric locomotives, hauling 12 ore trucks. The passenger service was maintained at a 15min frequency with five cars, increased to 10min on Fridays and Saturdays. On Saturdays, when everyone went shopping and there were rugby football fixtures, every car was pressed into service and it was not uncommon for 100 passengers to crowd on to the double deckers, the stairways and gangways packed tight, with people standing on the buffers and clinging to platform dashes. There were 1d (0.42p) intermediate stages, with a through fare of 4d (2p) single, 7d (3p) return. After the cessation of passenger services in 1927, freight trains continued until 1934 when an aerial ropeway was constructed. The company's electric generating station continued to supply street lighting and power for industrial and domestic purposes until nationalised in 1948. The tramway poles are still used for electric light standards.

In November 1927 the Devon and Cornwall Motor Transport Companies were sold to National; in seven short years a legend and a tradition had been created and to this day the former employees still meet annually. Those who so glibly speak of modern progress in the 1970s, both employers and employees, might do well to consider the examples of the GWR road motor department and of the DMT in the context both of enterprise and staff loyalty; things do not always get better and human material can degenerate just as surely as less animate materials.

Early Days in Plymouth 1880–1930

Plymouth is a complex urban area, consisting originally of three separate local authorities, Plymouth, Devonport and Stonehouse. It is not surprising that the early history of its internal transport system is equally complicated, revolving around several district tramway companies and the Corporation tramway system. First on the scene was the Plymouth, Stonehouse & Devonport Tramway Co in 1870, which despite its comprehensive title only succeeded in operating a horse tram service on standard gauge rails between Theatre Royal, Plymouth, and Cumberland Gardens, Devonport (opened in 1872 and extended to Marlborough Street in 1874); nevertheless it could claim to have some lengths of line in Plymouth, Stonehouse and Devonport. This was followed in 1880 by the Plymouth, Devonport & District Tramways Co, which not unnaturally found itself at loggerheads with the earlier company. Considerable argument ensued but the situation was finally solved by lack of capital on the part of the later company which constructed a line between Millbay Station, Plymouth, and Mannamead via Mutley, serving a totally different part of the urban area from the first company. The service was opened in 1884 with five steam hauled trams, which barely survived a year before being withdrawn as unreliable. The line lay derelict for four years until a new company, Plymouth Tramways Co recommenced working in 1889 with horse trams. In 1892 it also ran into difficulties and was purchased by Plymouth Corporation for £12,500; this was the first appearance of the Corporation as a transport operator in Plymouth. By now, the concept of a tramway was becoming accepted as an essential component of the life of any large town. The Corporation applied themselves with energy to the reconstruction of the line with extensions southward to West Hoe and northward to Compton Lane; the remodelled system, still horse drawn, was reopened in April 1893 and several extensions followed during the ensuing three years. Electrification was started in 1899 and completed by 1901; in the latter year the original tramway (Plymouth, Stonehouse & Devonport Co) was purchased by Plymouth and Devonport Corporations, electrified and then leased back to the company for a 21 year period, because of local authority boundary complications.

Another company, the BET-owned Devonport & District Tramways Co, came on the scene in 1901 and put into operation 20 double deck cars built in the USA by J. G. Brill Co on five routes wholly within Devonport. To complicate the position still further, between 1900 and 1903 Devonport Corporation laid $3\frac{1}{2}$ miles of tramway from Camels Head to Saltash Passage and from Keyham to Peverell which it decided to lease to the Devonport & District Tramways Co. This tramway was short lived, as the amalgamation of the three towns in 1914 at last gave Plymouth Corporation the powers to establish a unified transport system within the urban complex. The Devonport & District Tramways Co was purchased in 1915, the necessary tramway links at Pennycomequick and Peverell were constructed and through running commenced in October 1916. The original and last remaining tramway company (the Plymouth, Stonehouse & Devonport) finally came into municipal ownership in 1922, on expiry of the 21 year lease.

Against this complex background of horse and electric trams, R. Baskerville had been running horse buses and four-in-hand coach trips to the surrounding country and moorland from 1890. In 1900 Plymouth Motor Co put into operation five Daimler cars on a route between the Clock Tower and Salisbury Road, probably the first attempt at any form of motorised public transport in the West. In 1910 an offer to provide privately owned buses in the town was refused by Plymouth Corporation and the electric tram reigned supreme within Plymouth until 1920. The Corporation than obtained its first motorbuses, (20 Straker Squire 31-seaters) which were operated on four routes not served by trams; 1923 saw the tramways at their fullest extent with 13 services in operation, but from this time onward the scales were tipped in favour of the motorbus. In 1924 further buses were purchased and additional routes introduced, while between 1925 and 1927 no fewer than 57 buses were obtained (Burford, Shelvoke and Drewry, Guy and AEC makes) a number being one-man operated. By 1927, ten routes were being run, all to districts not served by tramcars. The following year saw the establishment of the present headquarters of the undertaking at Milehouse, in premises of the former Devonport & District Tramways.

By the late 1920s the tramway track and rolling stock had reached a state where large scale repairs and replacements were necessary and these factors, coupled with a heavy debt incurred by the trams, led the Corporation to decide on a ten year conversion programme to buses, commencing in 1930.

Although buses were inhibited by electric trams in Plymouth, the motor char-a-banc was having a field day. The first char-a-banc to appear was operated by A. C. Turner's Tours (later acquired by the DMT in 1924); it was a 28 seat Karrier vehicle powered by a 60hp Tyler engine, performing six miles per gallon, with solid tyres, folding hood, oil burning lamps and a 45 gallon petrol tank! With such a large population to draw upon, other char-a-bancs quickly followed; there were Violets, Roses, Silvers, Palaces, Norah, Charmaine, Prince, Princesses, Gliders and Eddystone. One can only assume that ungainly, ugly girls were all the rage in those days! These were all owner driver char-a-bancs, but in addition there was the more stolid Embankment Motor Co which continued as the only independent tour operator in Plymouth until 1974 when it was purchased by Wallace Arnold Tours Ltd. Because of the low speed limit (12mph) some of the longer day trips were marathons; the Land's End tour left at 6.30am and returned home at midnight— provided there were no breakdowns, or rainstorms which required everyone to dismount and help put up the hood!

The owner-driver char-a-bancs resorted to all manner of ruses to obtain passengers; for example, each owner would put up boards for four or five different tours, directing all his clients to one vehicle, then when everyone was ready to go, there would be a general exchange between all operators— everyone was satisfied and a small thing like hopping out of one chara into another was all part of the game. Then there were the 'chinks'—friends and relations of the driver, who would sit in the coach to give the gullible public the impression that this was a very popular tour, almost full up and ready to start. Touting, ie shouting the virtues of one's coach and tour on the pavement and button holing passengers, was the accepted order of the day.

Thus we come to the end of these cock-a-hoop, romantic days, when, with sufficient drive, one could create a bus empire in two or three years, or just have a lark with one of those new fangled petrol machines named after the favourite girl friend. After 1929/30, the bus industry grew up, became much more serious, much more important, much more a matter for professionals, but it lost its sense of fun and gallantry.

(*above*) Southern National 377 at Ilfracombe, an ECW bodied 1939 L type rebuild. New to Eastern Counties it came via Lincolnshire to the SNOC in 1954. (A O Watkins); (*below*) No 1611, an ECW/Bristol LWL5G at Lands End in 1967. (A O Watkins)

(*above*) One of the Southern National's few Bristol MW saloons working on the Bideford – Exeter service in 1966. (A O Watkins); (*below*) few KS Bristols were built, and even fewer were bought by Western National. One of three Bristol engined versions in the fleet was No 1812 seen here at St Ives. (*A O Watkins*)

3 Western and Southern National and Plymouth Corporation

Upon their formation on 1 January 1929, Western National and Southern National found themselves overnight the possessors of one of the most extended territories in Great Britain, with services stretching from Cheltenham in the north east and Bournemouth in the south east right through to Land's End in the west. It was a territory serving portions of seven counties, over 200 miles from east to west and involving a fleet of 518 vehicles (340 Western National and 178 Southern National) of many different types and makes. There remained many smaller operators and large gaps in the continuity of Western and Southern National territory. In these circumstances it is not surprising that the first ten years of the companies' histories consisted of an intensive process of purchasing and absorbing some 100 small operators.

During the first two years of their existence, until May 1931, the two new companies were fully occupied in organising themselves and sorting out their heterogenous fleet. The head office continued at the National premises at 206 Brompton Road, London with local control through two managers, one at Yeovil and one at Plymouth. During this interim period, relatively few acquisitions of local operators were made, four in the Southern National's North Devon area (Hodges Motor Services, Combe Martin; Bushell, Clovelly; A. Braund, Braunton; F. W. Squires, Barnstaple) and three in Western National territory. Most significant of the latter was the West Penwith Motor Co Ltd of St Just which operated on the Penzance—St Just route, and Palace Saloon

(J. G. S. Pullen) of Plymouth, which ran the important suburban services between Plymouth, Plymstock (via Pomphlett and
via Dean Cross) and Hooe, which are now part of the Plymouth Joint Services network. The other Western National
acquisition was E. E. Piper, Devizes. The timetables for 1929
clearly show the state of transition, for although Western
and Southern National were formed in February of that
year, the timetable for December was still published as
National services in Devon and Cornwall, comprising the
former DMT, CMT, Hardy-Colwill and National routes
but excluding the GWR road services. The latter continued
to be published as separate booklets entitled GWR—National
for three separate areas, West Cornwall, East Cornwall and
Devon. From the beginning of 1930 the position was clarified
to the extent that all Western National services in South
Devon and Cornwall were brought together in one timetable.
It was not until five years later that the six operating areas
of Western and Southern National, which continued until
recent years, were finalised. Experiments were also made with
fleet livery at this time, in an effort to discriminate between
Western, Southern and Eastern National and for a brief
period Western National vehicles appeared in a gloomy
maroon and cream. This was soon abandoned, and green
and cream was adopted for both Western and Southern
National. This livery continued in use until it was replaced
on vehicles with the National Bus Company's corporate
colours and style in the 1970s.

Meanwhile, a new competitor emerged at Plymouth with
the registration of H. B. Buses Ltd on 17 March 1929,
followed in eight days by the establishment of a subsidiary at
Redruth, Cornish Buses Ltd. This new operator took over
the old established service of Messrs Hopper & Berryman
between Plymouth, Plympton and Ivybridge, and before
long had introduced a Plymouth-Torquay service in competition with the Devon General-National joint route, and a

Plymouth-Hooe service acquired from Eddystone Motor Tours (W. J. Coath & Son) in competition with the former Palace Saloon route. Cornish Buses Ltd also started a service from Plymouth to Penzance via Tavistock, Liskeard, St Austell, Truro and Camborne, and Western National countered with a Plymouth-Truro service. However, the crucial battle was fought out on the Camborne-Redruth route, with all the classic devices of the pirate bus, until local people became alarmed at the dangers of racing on the road and the two parties settled down to an agreed 10min frequency. Cornish Buses also succeeded in establishing themselves jointly with Western National on the Truro-Falmouth road. These powerful competitors had the backing of the Mumford family, who had been established as coach builders in Plymouth since 1900.

After starting with the construction of horse-drawn carriages and buses, Mumfords turned to the motor car business in 1903. By 1912 the company owned a number of taxi cabs and started to operate char-a-bancs under the name Purple Tours. But from 1915, body building became its main activity and it built many char-a-bancs and saloon buses, including a number for Plymouth Corporation Transport Department and Western/Southern National. It continued in this field until World War II, after which the firm concentrated on its motoring interests and ceased building. bus bodies. Its business was obviously so successful that it sought other outlets in 1929 by the investment in H. B. Buses and Cornish Buses. In September, 1929 Western National came to terms with this vigorous new operator by the establishment of agreed joint services between Plymouth and Torquay (making a third party with Devon General) and on the group of services from Plymouth to Elburton, Hooe and Wembury.

Early in 1930, another of the great pioneers of bus services, J. H. Watts of the Red & White group, began to take an interest in this rapidly expanding operator and H. B. Buses was reformed as Southern General Omnibus Co Ltd, Plymouth, with both Mr C. Mumford and Mr J. H. Watts on the board. This new company brought a strange and quick reaction from the London General Omnibus Co which jealous for its name, immediately registered Western, Northern and Eastern General Omnibus Companies to stop anyone else stepping in, even though none of these companies ever owned a bus or turned a wheel! The Southern General and Cornish Buses enterprise was short lived, being bought out by Western National in November 1931, but during their 2½ years of life, a fleet of 40 buses and 25 coaches had been built up, most with bodies specially constructed by Mumfords, all but 11 on AEC chassis. These buses were well in advance of their time, with front entrance and one-man operated folding doors. The livery was prussian blue, with a darker blue waist band and white roofs and pillars.

With the elimination of Southern General, Western National had almost a monopoly (apart from Plymouth Corporation) of bus services within a 15 mile arc on the Devon side of the Tamar. Three independent operators remained: Embankment Motor Co which operated between Plymouth, Buckland Monachorum and Dousland, Zenith Bus Service (E. V. Lowe) which ran between Plymouth and Mothecombe with additional local journeys between Plymouth and Yealmpton, and Star Motor Service (J. W. Newton & Son) which ran between Plymouth, Heybrook Bay and Wembury Point and which later became Heybrook Bay Motor Services Ltd. In July, 1930 the GWR withdrew passenger services on the Plymouth-Yealmpton branch line and Western National introduced an increased bus service.

Meanwhile Plymouth Corporation, under the guidance of its new general manager Mr Clem Jackson who was to remain in charge of the undertaking for nearly 30 years, standardised its fleet livery to an immaculate maroon lined in gold, with cream roofs and pillars lined in red. In October, 1930 the first stage of the tramway replacement was effected, six Leyland TD1s taking over from tramcars on the Devonport-Saltash Passage route.

During this stormy two years for Western National, the affairs of Southern National continued at a more tranquil level. In North Devon the administration of the area was concentrated on Bideford and 1929 saw the introduction of the first covered-top double-deckers in the area, when Leyland Titan TD1 commenced on the trunk route between Ilfracombe and Westward Ho! via Barnstaple and Bideford (service 301). In the Somerset and Dorset area services continued to be concentrated on the ex National depots at Yeovil, Bridport, Weymouth and Portland, with administrative headquarters at Yeovil. Dorset was (and still is) a difficult territory from the point of view of bus operation, because of the sparse overall population.

The years 1930/1 also saw the introduction of inter-availability of tickets between road and rail, first on the Taunton-Minehead route, to counteract the activities of independent operators, and then on a much wider basis in April 1931 on long distance express coach services between London and 16 popular holiday resorts in the South West. This was the first example in the country of the interchange of tickets between rail and long distance express coach services.

The years 1931–9 formed a period of rapid expansion. Thomas Tilling Ltd, the new owners of Western/Southern National which took over control in May 1931 were no newcomers to the business of running buses and immediately set about reorganising, consolidating and expanding its large new subsidiaries in the South West.

Tillings recognised that the management of a large transport undertaking could best be carried out on the spot and in May 1932, the old National headquarters at 206 Brompton Road were closed and the head offices of Western and

Southern National established at 48/50 Queen Street, Exeter. Exeter was chosen as the most central point for the administration of the two companies' large territory, although it placed them in the unique position of having a head office situated in the operating territory of another bus company (Devon General). It was also realised that two area managers could not cope with such a widespread and rapidly growing business and during May 1933 six operating areas were established, each with an area traffic superintendent and an area engineer. The areas were designated Cornwall, South Devon and East Cornwall, Somerset and East Devon, Gloucester and Wiltshire, Somerset and Dorset, North Devon and North Cornwall (the last two being Southern National).

Western and Southern National found themselves the inheritors of a fleet consisting of vehicles of a wide variety of makes, types and sizes. This not only resulted in excessive storage space for spare parts and units, but also greatly complicated the work of fitters and engineering staff generally. It was obviously desirable that some form of standardisation should take place, particularly to the Tilling group, whose policy elsewhere was to standardise largely on the Bristol chassis in which it had a financial interest. Accordingly in 1932, a Bristol C double decker was loaned to Western National and was used on the busy service between Plymouth and Plympton (service 87). The experiment proved satisfactory and in 1933 Western National took delivery of 9 Bristol H single-deckers, all with Bristol bodies, but Southern National took delivery at the same time of 16 TSM B39 single-deckers with Brush bodies. During the years preceding World War II standardisation on Bristol single-deckers was gradually completed, except for services requiring small vehicles for which Dennis Ace and Mace buses were obtained. The first eight Bristol coaches were taken into the fleet in March 1935 for use between London and Bournemouth on the newly acquired Royal Blue express services. It was not until 1937, however, that Bristol double deckers made their appearance, the first being ten of the new oil engined GO5G models (five-cylinder Gardner engines) with Beadle high-bridge bodies. Those vehicles were allocated to urban routes with heavy traffic, six to service 33 Camborne-Redruth (Western National) and four to service 22 Radipole-Weymouth-Portland (Southern National). At this time permission could not be obtained to operate double deckers further south from Weymouth than Portland (Victoria Square) because of the steep hill and elbow bend overlooking the sea on the road to Easton, Southwell and Portland Bill. Six Leyland Tiger TS7D six wheeled single deckers were obtained and maintained the service satisfactorily for many years—the only six wheelers in the Western or Southern National fleet. It was not until 1969 that Bristol double deckers were finally put into service south of Victoria Square, Portland. In 1937, a further ten Bristol double deckers on the new K5G type chassis were obtained, eight going to Plymouth for use on Service 87 Plymouth-Plympton and 95 Plymouth-Hooe and the remaining two to Weymouth for use on Service 22.

The 1930s saw a considerable expansion and acquisition of local operators; a complete list of the businesses absorbed will be found in Appendix B. During the period under discussion 87 local operators were acquired, 37 by Western National and 50 by Southern National. But 1932 was rather quiet, for it brought no startling developments; Southern National purchased three operators in its Somerset and Dorset area, the most significant being Chaplin & Rogers of Chard, as it represented the first move westward from the old National depots of Yeovil, Weymouth and Bridport. Western National acquired only one operator that year,.

In contrast 1933 was a busy year, 26 operators being purchased, the most important of which was the joint

Southern/Western National acquisition of the express services of Highways Ltd of London W1. This operator had commenced a London-Plymouth service in 1928 and followed in 1931 with London-Newquay, London-Bournemouth-Plymouth and London-Ilfracombe; its acquisition brought 20 coaches into the Western/Southern National fleet, 17 of the very latest type of Gilfords. The purchase of Highways was a key move towards the much bigger prize of Elliott Bros (Bournemouth) Royal Blue services, two years later. Among the Western National 1933 acquisitions were Zenith Bus Service, Plymouth and the stage services of Embankment Motor Co Plymouth (its tour activities continued under Embankment control). A general tidying-up of timetables in the Plymouth area ensued, with a regular hourly frequency to Dousland and Buckland Monachorum, and a one third reduction on the Yealmpton road where competing interests had led to a too frequent service. There were also three important acquisitions in the Taunton area during 1933, Thomas Motors Ltd (Lavender Blue) of Taunton, P. G. Hanks of Bishops Lydeard and Dunns Motor Services, Taunton. Mr Hanks had run a horse bus service between Taunton and Bishops Lydeard and it was only after World War I that he went over to motor bus operation. By 1925 Hanks buses were also serving Fitzhead and Cothelstone, largely by pirating the efforts of C. Withers, whose story as a motorbus pioneer in the area north of Taunton will be told later. The Western National acquisition of Hanks was not all that successful, as Mr Withers strenuously opposed the grant of licences to Fitzhead and Cothelstone and was successful in his case before the Traffic Commissioners; nevertheless, Western National had strengthened its hold on the important Taunton-Bishops Lydeard section.

Thomas Motors Ltd had originally started in 1910 as Thomas' Posting Establishment Ltd and built up an important taxi cab business within Taunton, together with char-a-banc excursions in the summer. After the war Mr Thomas commenced a daily facility between Taunton and Minehead and changed the name of the business in July 1928 to Thomas Motors Ltd operating under the fleet name of Lavender Blue. At this time both Thomas Motors and National were working daily services on the Taunton-Minehead road, the latter company through the acquisition of Hardy Central Garage Co Ltd which had operated on this route since 1923. The following year, 1929, a third operator appeared on the Minehead road, Mr E. J. Dunn of Taunton; the position by 1932 on this main route out of Taunton was five journeys per day by Dunn, four by Western National, five by Lavender Blue, plus 6 to 18 per day by Hanks locally to Bishops Lydeard, and services by C. Withers from Taunton to Fitzhead, Cothelstone and Bagborough. It was obvious that so great a variety of operators could not continue economically and the Western National acquisitions of 1933 swept the board, with the exception of C. Withers, whose facilities continued until 1952. The frequency of the Taunton-Minehead route was reduced from hourly to every 90min and between Taunton and Bishops Lydeard from half hourly to every 45min. A further reduction to two hourly and hourly respectively was made in 1935.

In 1934, Southern National acquired R. Deacon, trading as Dorchester Motor Services and the purchase gave it a depot in Dorchester together with local routes which have developed over the years into the present useful town network; excursions and tours from Dorchester were also included in the transaction. Western National absorbed five operators in 1934, the most important being Way, Goodall & Lord, trading as Dartmouth & District Bus Co; 1934 also marked the end of railway-operated bus services, when the GWR handed over to Southern National its Radipole-Weymouth-Wyke Regis service. It was also the year in which the isolated pockets inherited by Western National from the GWR at Bovey Tracey and Moretonhampstead were transferred to Devon General, which was the major operator in the territory concerned.

A year later, 1935, was another period of rapid, large scale expansion, with 14 operators taken over by Southern National and six by Western National. The acquisition of two operators in Lyme Regis (A. T. Baker, Pride of Lyme, and Mrs E. M. Watson) gave the company its Lyme Regis depot, while the purchase of Reynolds Bros of Padstow provided a new depot in the North Devon and North Cornwall area. This year also saw the closure of the Lynton & Barnstaple narrow gauge railway line, and Southern National purchased two special vehicles with large lockers at the rear for the carriage of mails and other goods, to replace the rail service.

But it was in the field of express coach services that the year 1935 was most significant for the two National companies, when they jointly acquired Elliott Bros (Bournemouth) Ltd, proprietors of Royal Blue Services. Over 100 coaches were involved in the purchase, which, together with their existing services made the two National companies owners of the largest network of express coach services in Great Britain. Royal Blue had commenced as early as 1880, with horsedrawn coaches, but by 1914 the entire fleet was motorised and in 1926 Royal Blue owned 72 coaches and 38 private hire cars, with five garages in Bournemouth. During the late 1920s, the standard of comfort and reliability of motor coaches had reached a point where the large scale expansion of long distance services was possible. Elliott Bros was quick to seize the opportunity and in 1928/9 services were started from Bournemouth to Plymouth, Ilfracombe, Birmingham, Margate and Bristol and from London to Plymouth and Weston-super-Mare (via Bristol). They were followed in 1930 by services from Southsea, Plymouth and

Ilfracombe to Birmingham. The Road Traffic Act of 1930 was followed by many intense and important legal battles in the traffic courts, as the Royal Blue routes were hotly contested by other operators; in one year £7,000 was spent in legal expenses. Nevertheless, with the help of some of the leading advocates of the time, Royal Blue won through and went on in 1932/3 to establish important co-ordination agreements with other operators.

At this time Traveller Saloon Coaches of Plymouth were acquired, with services from Portsmouth to Plymouth and Bristol. In 1934 Royal Blue had the distinction of taking delivery of the first AEC Q type vehicle to be put on the road, the first full fronted coach with the engine at the side instead of in the conventional front position. During this year Royal Blue was also an active participant in the formation of Associated Motorways, a partnership of limited liability companies, based on Cheltenham with revenue allocated in proportion to the percentage of mileage operated by each member company. Towards the end of 1934 the two Elliott Brothers decided to sell at the peak of their success, a measure of which is provided by the fact that, after acquisition, Western/Southern National decided to retain the trading name of Royal Blue for all their express services. For over 90 years coaches bearing the fleet name Royal Blue have been on the roads of Southern England—probably the oldest continuous trading name in the history of British road passenger transport. The excursions and tours side of Elliott Bros' business was transferred to Hants & Dorset Motor Services, Bournemouth and did not pass to Western/ Southern National.

The story of expansion in the express service field does not end with Elliott Bros and in May, 1935, the important business of Tourist Motor Coaches (Southampton) Ltd was purchased, with 24 vehicles. This had been founded in 1919 by Mr B. H. Ransom, who operated motor char-a-banc tours. One of these was a regular tour from Southampton to London, which in 1927 developed into a daily express coach service. In 1930 one journey was extended via Bournemouth to Exeter, Torquay and Plymouth. Tourist had the distinction of starting the first night service in the South West—a Friday night coach in July and August from Southampton to Torquay. The business continued to grow and in 1930 Tourist also commenced the long express route from Southampton to Warrington and Liverpool, which by 1933 had been extended to Bournemouth and operated daily during August. In 1935 Southern National acquired Greyhound Coaches (Weymouth) Ltd, comprising excursions and tours from Weymouth, and a Portland-Portsmouth express service (mainly for naval ratings), and also the business of A. E. Good (Silver Cars), Seaton, which operated a London-Bournemouth-Exmouth express service. The rapid acquisitions of express service operators presented the two National companies with quite an administrative problem and they immediately set to work to merge the various services and simplify timetables. Readers seeking more detailed information of express service developments should consult the *History of Royal Blue Express Services* published by David & Charles, though now out of print.

In 1936 the two companies purchased 12 operators; of these four were in North Devon, including the important excursions and tours business and London-Ilfracombe seasonal express service of Scarlet Pimpernel Cars & Motor Supplies Ltd, Ilfracombe but all the remainder were in the Somerset & Dorset area and marked the infilling of the western portion of that area based on Chard and Seaton. At Chard the important business of F. Sully & Sons (Sully's Services) was jointly acquired by Southern and Western National, while in the Seaton area Southern National purchased T. H. Clapp of Seaton, F. W. Dowell of Branscombe and C. R. Good (Pioneer) of Beer. Three small operators jointly trading as Portland Express were also obtained in the Weymouth area.

By 1937 the impetus was slackening, due largely to the fact that the number of small operators available for purchase was greatly reduced. The two companies acquired seven operators, the most important being Bartlett & Nicholls (Blue County Cars) of Langton Matravers, which led to the establishment of a depot at Swanage. Of the remaining small operators bought in 1937, five were in the Southern National Somerset & Dorset area (Miles & Lee of Coombe St Nicholas, Chard, being a joint acquisition with Western National) and one in the Western National Somerset & East Devon area.

The purchases in 1938 accounted for six operators, the most important being Truscott Bros of Rillamill, Callington, which resulted in the opening of a small depot at Launceston. By the end of 1938 the final pattern of depots and sub depots had been established, with the exception of Delabole, which was a post-war addition. The business of S. T. Heard & Son (Red Deer Coaches) of Timberscombe near Minehead, was also acquired during this year; its maroon buses with a deer's head on the side, provided services from Minehead to the Exmoor villages of Wheddon Cross, Exford, Winsford and Simonsbath and were very popular with holidaymakers in the summer. In 1971 these services were reduced to Minehead-Wheddon Cross only, because of the general decline in rural bus services. An experiment in conjunction with Somerset County Council to resume the moorland section of route beyond Wheddon Cross on one day per week, failed after 12 months because of a lack of adequate support.

With the clouds of war gathering in 1939, and the prevailing general uncertainty, acquisitions were down to four—the tours business of Edwards at Bude for Southern National and three operators in Cornwall for Western National, the

83

important one being T. W. Billinghurst of Saltash with local services from that town.

Express services had also shown a lively expansion during the years 1936–9; through running between Bournemouth and Brighton jointly with Southdown was commenced in July 1936, while in 1937/8 Royal Blue inclusive holidays in the South and West were inaugurated with coach travel to and from London, hotel accommodation and local tours. In 1937 the Royal Blue network into Cornwall was extended and a combined coach/air service from London to the Isle of Wight via Eastleigh aerodrome was inaugurated, one of the earliest such arrangements in Great Britain. The following year a new cross country express service was introduced from Bridport to Bristol, while in 1939 non stop express journeys were in operation from London to Bournemouth (Channel Coast Express), Exeter (Cornish Coast Express), Minehead (Minehead Express) and Weymouth (Weymouth Bay Express). It is clear that Western/Southern National were continuing the spirit of enterprise and innovation in the express service field, so ably started by the Elliott Brothers.

Apart from the acquisition of local operators, the 1930s were characterised by an expansion in bus traffic generally. The bus had become established as a reliable and comfortable means of moving about and people, who had for centuries remained static in towns and villages. now had available, at a relatively low cost, the means of visiting the seaside, the country, towns for shopping, football and sporting fixtures, journeys to friends and relations. The private car was still a comparatively rare possession of the middle and upper classes of society. The pattern of expansion was general throughout the territories of Western and Southern National: a new depot at Bridgwater to house 15 vehicles, the replacement of single-deckers by double-deckers on all the main services in North Devon (Ilfracombe to Westward Ho!, Combe Martin and Woolacombe;

Barnstaple to Croyde and Georgeham; Bideford to Clovelly and Bude), the establishment of long distance cross-country services (eg Ilfracombe-Newquay, Plymouth-Bideford, Plymouth-Bude, Exeter-Bideford), together with the long distance developments in South Devon mentioned in detail in Chapter 4. There were also local extensions and the opening up of new routes (eg St Mawes-Truro via King Harry Ferry, Plymouth-Crownhill-Bowden Cross, and extensions from Looe to Hannafore). The buoyant mood of the industry also brought its problems and during 1936/7 there were hard fought battles in the traffic courts with Plymouth Corporation over new and increased services in and around the city, together with disputes over protective fares for the Corporation undertaking within the old City boundary, wrangles which were not properly solved until the introduction of the Joint Services scheme in 1942. There were also sensible moves in this period to consolidate and rationalise routes which had tended to become over served in the earlier days of unrestricted competition; in 1935 the Camborne-Redruth service was reduced from 10 to 12min frequency and St Austell-Truro-Camborne-Penzance was established on a regular hourly basis. Behind the scenes from 1936 onward was the steady conversion of vehicles from petrol to the more reliable and cheaper oil propulsion, the larger diesel unit in front sometimes necessitating the reduction of the length of the rear platform by a few inches in order to comply with the maximum length restrictions.

Meanwhile, during the period 1931-9, Plymouth Corporation was continuing its tramway replacement policy and in 1931 the Theatre-West Hoe service was withdrawn. Leyland TD1s and Dennis Lancet buses were purchased during this year, but so also were nine open top double-deck tramcars, taken over from Exeter Corporation when its tram system was closed down. The following year, the Theatre-Compton tramway was converted to bus operation and 38 Leyland

TD2s and three Dennis Lancet double deck buses were taken into the fleet. Nevertheless, in 1933–4 we again find Plymouth Corporation acquiring tramcars, this time six bogie and six single truck cars from Torquay Tramways Co. The Theatre-Royal Naval Barracks tram route was closed in 1934, 14 Leyland TD3 buses being purchased to replace the trams. In 1935 the Corporation decided to reconstitute its bus fleet by the elimination of single deckers; to replace them, 37 gearless Leylands (the first oil engined buses in the Plymouth fleet) were acquired and enabled the Milehouse-Stoke-Devonport tram route to be closed. A year later saw the withdrawal of trams between Drake Circus and Prince Rock, the bus fleet being further augmented by 37 Leyland Titans (gearless). At the beginning of 1937 Prince Rock tram depot was closed and the tramcars scrapped. A further batch of 14 gearless Titans was purchased during that year, allowing the abandonment of the two circular tram routes (Theatre-Wilton Street-Fore Street-Theatre, and Theatre-Peverell-Milehouse-Fore Street-Theatre). During 1937 all the bus routes were numbered. To complete the pre-war picture a further 25 gearless Leyland Titans were purchased bringing the fleet at the end of 1939 to 206 Leylands (144 oil engined), seven Dennis Lancets, two Leyland Cubs and one AEC Regent; thirty bus routes were in operation and one tram service remained on which 13 single truck trams were used.

So ended a period of solid and satisfying achievement, perhaps lacking the flair and romance of the 1920s but attaining more in terms of real value and service to the community. By 1939 Great Britain possessed the most comprehensive and intensive road passenger system in the world, but in human affairs nothing is static and no trend can continue indefinitely and the pattern built up so painstakingly during the 1930s was rudely and irrevocably broken by the outbreak of World War II.

(*above*) A pre-production Lodekka, No 1863, waits at The Lizard before return-ing to Helston. (*A O Watkins*); (*below*) the first of Western National's Bristol SUS4As, No 600, draws out of Penzance bus station shortly before Christmas 1968. (*A O Watkins*)

(*above*) A wet day in summer 1965 and SUL coach No 402 pauses in Lynton on a private hire working. (*A O Watkins*); (*below*) two of the rare Bedford/ECW buses built for the NBC in 1967 were Western National Nos 701 and 702 pictured at Kingsbridge in 1970. (*A O Watkins*)

The impact of the War was sudden and total, though not altogether unexpected. For several months before the outbreak of hostilities the companies had been drawing up plans for drastic reductions in timetables to meet the requirements of fuel rationing in the event of war and numbers of vehicles had been earmarked for military purposes. These plans were put into immediate operation in September,1939 and marked a complete reversal of the policies of the preceding eight years. Instead of being developed, services were cut to cater for essential needs only; all summer holiday routes were temporarily abandoned, together with the augmentations of basic services during the holiday season. By 1940, scheduled mileage had been reduced by 40 per cent although at some depots, for example Bridgwater and Torpoint, there was a build up of vehicles compared with pre war, to meet the expanded needs of the Royal Ordnance Factory and naval establishments respectively. The acquisition of local operators halted completely, as no one could foresee the future or gauge the value of a business under wartime conditions. It was a case of all operators, large and small, pooling resources in the national interest and employing buses and coaches for whatever purposes the government deemed fit. Delivery of new vehicles ceased, as the chassis and body manufacturers converted their premises to armament production and it was necessary for bus companies to extemporise, as best they could. In addition, 58 vehicles were requisitioned by the military and a further 39 were converted to ambulances. Moreover, petrol rationing for private cars was very stringent indeed, with the result that a great volume of extra traffic was thrown on to the reduced bus services; standing passenger regulations were relaxed and rapidly aging fleets of buses conveyed abnormal loads in abnormal conditions of blackout and later of enemy air attack. Express services continued, but on a greatly reduced basis and Royal Blue was responsible for evacuating nearly 28,000 passengers from London to the safe areas of the South West. But as the military position worsened and fuel rationing became more severe, express services finally ceased in November 1942, and the Royal Blue network, built up so carefully for 60 years, came to a halt; it was not quite a total halt, as the Ministry of Transport realised that certain cross country coach routes were indispensable and six long distance stage services were authorised.

The toll of war made itself felt more directly than by shortage and restrictions and it was not long before the two National companies were involved in enemy air attack. In August, 1940 the roof of Portland garage was damaged by bomb blast and two months later the Southern National main garage in Weymouth received a direct hit; four employees were killed and 14 vehicles severely damaged. In November, 1940 two Southern National buses on hire to the army at Houndstone Camp, Yeovil, were completely destroyed and a Royal Blue coach on service had a miraculous escape when a bomb dropped immediately behind it on Putney Heath; the coach was blown off the road but apart from shock and bruises everyone survived. The following months, Plymouth began to feel the weight of air attacks and just after Christmas a number of incendiary bombs fell round a bus in service; the conductress showed great courage and took all her passengers to shelter just before the bus burst into flames and was destroyed.

Plymouth achieved the unenviable record of becoming Britain's third most bombed town (after London and Hull) and it was here that the company suffered its most serious losses. After minor damage in February, 1941, the garage and workshops received terrible blows in the devastating air raid of March 1941. They were literally reduced to a junk heap, with 53 vehicles badly damaged (11 of them beyond repair) and practically all workshop equipment and stores were completely destroyed, including records, tickets and uniforms. Despite herculean efforts by all staff to get things running again, an almost similar raid a month later brought all the endeavours to nought and the company reluctantly decided that it must transfer its central maintenance activities to Bideford, where Southern National already owned substantial premises. The move was made in May 1941, involving the use of many buses, heavy machinery transporters and the transfer of all staff into temporary accommodation 60 miles away from their Plymouth homes. During May, minor damage was sustained at Falmouth and Penzance garages. In August, 1941 a curious incident occurred in Cornwall when a bus carrying workmen to an airfield was struck by one of our own Spitfires and the roof carried away, leaving the occupants scared but unharmed! The company's vehicles and staff enjoyed a respite until April 1942, when vehicles on service at both Swanage and Falmouth were shot up by German fighter planes. Finally in April 1944, in almost the last air attack on Plymouth, the company's Laira Garage again received a direct hit causing serious damage and killing three employees on firewatching duties. During this raid a double decker completely vanished, leaving no fragment large enough to identify. The total toll of war on the company's vehicles was 23 completely destroyed and 121 seriously damaged.

During 1942/3 the site of the Western National works at Plymouth was used for the assembly of imported military vehicles for the American forces and similar activities took place in the second half of 1944 in preparation for the D-Day invasion of France. Altogether 1,000 vehicles were assembled at the works.

To combat the growing fuel shortage, the company turned its attentions to gas producer operation in 1942, and Taunton depot was made the centre for these activities. Tilling type 2T2 trailers were employed; they were, in effect, small anthracite burners producing combustible gas for feeding into the engine in place of petrol or diesel oil. Despite great technical ingenuity, these burners could only produce low efficiency fuel and they suffered from many defects including damage to valves and combustion chamber from the gas fuel. Nevertheless, altogether 55 vehicles were converted to gas operation. They worked regularly from Taunton to Burnham-on-Sea, Wellington, Chard, Minehead and Yeovil as well as on Taunton town services; the Bridgwater-Minehead and Barnstaple-Westward Ho! services were also maintained by gas propelled buses and a few even worked on Royal Blue coach services. Altogether ¼ million gallons of fuel were saved by this method, though gas producer vehicles were quickly abandoned when the war ceased.

The other important wartime development was brought about directly by the bombing of Plymouth. Not only was Western National sustaining losses but also Plymouth Corporation's Milehouse depot was severely damaged in the April 1941 raids, and a number of buses destroyed and damaged. But even more damaging to the Corporation's undertaking was the loss of passengers, as people moved out from the city to the comparative safety of the surrounding rural area. As a result, Western National found itself with a depleted fleet and a greatly increased passenger potential while the Corporation found itself with a depleted fleet but an even more depleted number of passengers resulting in a deficit in its accounts. The two concerns therefore took the only sensible course and after careful negotiations established the Plymouth Joint Services co-ordinated area on 1 October 1942. This area is bounded on the west by the River Tamar and on the north and east by a line through Buckland Monachorum, Yelverton, Dousland, Shaugh Prior, Cornwood, Plympton, Elburton and Wembury; within the area all transport is pooled on the basis of 80 per cent of mileage and receipts to the corporation and 20 per cent to Western National. Under the new arrangement, corporation buses were permitted to operate outside the city boundary and

Western National buses were able to charge local fares and share in the town traffic. The scheme continues unchanged to the present day and has served as a model for joint transport arrangements elsewhere. Separate time and fare tables are issued for the Plymouth Joint Services area and the scale of fares has always differed from that applicable throughout the remainder of the Western/Southern National territories.

Fortunately for both Western National and Plymouth Corporation, wartime utility vehicles with wooden seats and painted grey mostly on Guy chassis, began to be delivered in 1942. During the last three years of the war, Plymouth Corporation took delivery of 113 such vehicles. The remaining tram route (Theatre-Peverell) was retained throughout the war, although the April 1941 air raids seriously disorganised it by bringing down much of the overhead equipment; car No 153 was totally destroyed near the Guildhall and car No 159 had its top deck destroyed in Milehouse depot and had to be scrapped. After repairs to the overhead, the service was curtailed at Drakes Circus and continued to operate from that terminal to Peverell until September 1945 when the tram system was closed down.

The end of hostilities in August 1945 found Western/ Southern National and Plymouth Corporation confronted with grave problems. Fuel and manpower were still extremely restricted and the recovery of vehicles from the military involved large scale repairs and rehabilitation. Nevertheless, the worst was over and barely a year had elapsed before new Bristol 'K' type buses were being delivered to the fleet. They were fitted with lowbridge Eastern Coach Works bodies and incorporated many improvements over pre war design; they were sturdy buses, which many people in retrospect regard as the best in bus design and performance. They had hard work to do, for the four or five post war years from 1945 to 1950 were the Indian Summer of bus operation. Freed from the anxieties of war but still with many of its restrictions, people wished to settle down and enjoy carefree holidays and days at the seaside or in the countryside. Within two years services were back to pre war levels and then followed a period of rapid expansion. These were the days when new services could be started up with the certainty of success and when existing well established services could be increased in frequency and still bring in handsome profits (eg the old National service 201 Taunton-Burnham-on-Sea was doubled from hourly to half hourly during this period). The West Country lanes were quiet and almost empty, and people enjoyed themselves soberly, before the avalanche of private cars, transistor radios, 'teles' and litter had debilitated the nation. The Bristol chassis works was unable to meet all demands for new buses and, as a result, in 1948, Western/ Southern National took delivery of 16 Leyland PD1As fitted with standard Eastern Coach Works bodies. In 1949, the pre-war Bristol GO5G vehicles were rehabilitated and brought up to date with new bodywork and lower mounted radiators similar to the new K type; these vehicles gave good service and continued in operation until 1957/8. By 1950 the Western/Southern National mileage was practically double the pre-war level and the route coverage was approaching its peak. Many routes had also been converted from single deck to double deck operation during this five year period.

Meanwhile, Royal Blue coach services recommenced, in skeleton form, on 1 April 1946. The skeleton put on flesh rapidly and by 1949 express services were back to pre-war level. The demand for long distance coaches had proved greater than anticipated and the stage was set for the rapid expansion which characterised coach services during the 1950s. Royal Blue had to make do with the old pre-war vehicles until the delivery in May 1948 of the new Bristol L6B and L6A vehicles, of which 45 were taken into the fleet by September 1949.

Plymouth Corporation too lost no time in renewing its war

94

worn fleet and in 1946 15 Leyland PD1 double deckers were delivered, followed early in 1947 by a further 35. The city itself began to stir from its ruins and new housing estates were built on the outskirts, some on very hilly terrain. New services to these estates required more powerful buses and in 1948 30 Leyland PD2s were acquired, together with six Crossley double deckers. At the same time, a portion of the old tram sheds at Milehouse was converted into a body works and extensive rebuilding of the wartime utility buses was effected. At the end of 1949 a further 35 Leyland PD2s were taken into the fleet and all buses acquired before 1938 were taken out of service. As the new Plymouth began to take shape, with well planned estates beyond the old city boundaries, the wisdom and foresight of the Plymouth Joint Services agreement was amply demonstrated, both company and corporation sharing in the new traffic without conflict or argument.

Acquisitions were virtually nil during this period, everyone was too busy rehabilitating their fleets and coping with the heavy traffic demands; for a relatively brief period, buses were a good line of business and no one was anxious to sell out. There were two minor exceptions, J. G. Mitchell of Creech St Michael, Taunton was purchased by Western National towards the end of 1945 and there was the sad case of Mr Martin of Truro, the bottom of whose bus fell out, so he turned over the operation of his Truro-St Day-Falmouth service to Western National at a moment's notice!

During this period, the first of the political moves affecting the industry took place. Tillings had always had keen businessmen at the helm and, taking advantage of the post war Labour Government which saw in public ownership a panacea for all human ills, they sold their entire bus empire to the British Transport Commission in 1948 while at the peak of its profitability and commanding a high price.

In 1950 a link with the past was severed by the closure of

the old GWR bus shed at Portscatho and the building of a new lock up garage a short distance away at Gerrans.

1950–70 The years of contraction

In many respects it is a pity that this history cannot end at 1950, with Western/Southern National at the peak of their achievement, and with more passengers, routes and buses than at any time before or since. But it is only the privilege of fiction to end happily ever after, and the sad duty of history to tell of anticlimax. In 1950 two events occurred, one of immense significance for the bus industry as a whole, and the other a straw in the wind for Western/Southern National. The important event was the final lifting of all fuel restrictions for private cars, which in its cumulative effects over the years has led to the closure of most rural railway branch lines and the gradual running down of public bus services, which are now faced with much the same fate as the railways. The smaller event was the tidying up exercise in the Stroud area, which resulted in Western National losing Stroud depot and 46 vehicles to Bristol Tramways & Carriage Co Ltd. It was not just a pity for sentimental reasons that the depot from which the old National originally established its foothold in the West should pass out of its control but it was also a significant pointer to the future.

However, in 1950 none of the shadows confronting the industry could be foreseen and, in fact, for a further three years everything continued very well for Western/Southern National, the peak fleet of 1,194 vehicles being reached in 1953. In that year new bus stations at Taunton and Truro were completed. With increasing road traffic and larger buses, it was becoming more difficult for public service vehicles to use town squares or side streets as terminal points and a more sophisticated travelling public grew to expect waiting rooms, cloak rooms and the other amenities afforded by central bus stations. These bus stations also enabled all services to terminate at one common point, to the advantage of both public and bus company, whereas before the war in certain towns (eg Plymouth) buses started from various terminals adjacent to the centre. In February 1953 the clearance of bomb damage and the start of reconstruction had proceeded far enough in Plymouth to permit the use of a cleared site off Union Street as a central terminus for all country services, pending the construction of a new, modern bus station at Breton Side.

The years 1952–3 were also marked by a final burst of buying out local operators when some small concerns, seeing the red light, chose to sell out on the best terms possible. The most notable was Blakes Bus Services Ltd of Delabole in 1952. This was the last acquisition of a completely new depot by the two National companies, or to be exact by Southern National acting under instructions from the British Transport Commission. Situated in the most sparsely populated area of North Cornwall, with services radiating to Plymouth, Bodmin, Launceston and Wadebridge, the depot never proved an economical proposition and was closed in 1971. The following year, Southern National also purchased Prout of Port Isaac, in the same thinly populated area. Western National purchases at this time were more fortunate and worthwhile; in 1952 Mr Foxworthy of Stoke Gabriel, trading as Dart Bus Service, was acquired, giving Western National a monopoly on the remunerative Stoke Gabriel-Paignton route. The same year also marked the purchase of the last remaining independent operator on the Taunton-Watchet road, Quantock Hauliers Ltd, with services from Taunton to Fitzhead, Cothelstone, Bagborough, Stogumber, and Williton. Quantock Hauliers had purchased the business from one of the earliest bus operators in Somerset, Mr C Withers, who started up immediately after the 1914–18 War with a 14-seat 8 cylinder Golbron Brillie vehicle on a route from Crowcombe to Taunton. He was in fact the first motor bus operator to and from Taunton, having commenced just before National set up its depot in Taunton. The acquisition by Western National of the other operators on the Taunton-Minehead road in the early 1930s enabled Mr Withers to develop in comparative peace in co-ordination with the big operator and by 1934 he had three vehicles, a fourth (Dennis Lancet) being added in 1938. With wartime evacuees, Mr Withers' traffic continued to expand and an extra vehicle was obtained (Bedford). The firm had a very good tradition of staff loyalty but was finally sold to Quantock Hauliers in 1945. In 1953 Western National purchased Porlock Blue Motors, with which it had operated a joint timetable on the Minehead-Porlock Weir route for many years, also Banfil & Barrington of Mawnan Smith, Cornwall.

On the express service side of the business, the years 1950–3 saw some important innovations, particularly the establishment of night journeys in 1951 on some six routes, initially to cater for people wishing to go to London for the Festival of Britain. These night runs proved so successful that they became a permanent feature of post war operation but they have declined in importance in recent years as a result of increased speeds made possible by the use of motorways. When it is appreciated that any towns or cities up to 200 miles apart, linked by motorway, involve a maximum of four hours running time it will be recognised that a journey which operated overnight can be completed during the evening or early morning.

But already adverse factors were beginning to take effect. Fares, which had remained static at pre war level (apart from express services, which were increased in 1946 and 1950), began to produce too little revenue to meet increasing costs, and in 1951 Western/Southern National were obliged to introduce their first all round increase on local bus fares. This was a new exercise altogether and while the Traffic Commissioners allowed a blanket increase (ie a fixed amount on each denomination of fare) they indicated that the inherited disparity in rates for similar distances was so great that any future increase must have some regard to mileage. Unfortunately future increases became almost an annual event; the inflationary trend was well under way, wage awards to operating staff came with monotonous regularity and declining passenger figures made it impossible to absorb extra costs without raising fares. To meet the Traffic Commissioners' wishes, fares were first put on some twelve different scales to fit the individual services, then on six area scales (one for each operating area of the companies), then on two scales and finally in 1957 on one standard scale applicable to all routes. In an area so essentially rural, no attempt was made to establish separate urban and rural scales, as is the case with many other bus companies; the local authorities in the West indicated that they would prefer one universal scale, so that there could be no question of town subsidising country or vice versa. In an effort to keep basic fares as cheap as possible, the companies gradually cut down concession fares over the years, finally abolishing all return tickets in 1967 and greatly reducing concession rates for scholars. With a traffic recession of 3–4 per cent per annum, fares have been increased on 34 occasions between 1951 and 1979 and are now approximately eight to nine times the pre-war level, which compares favourably with most other commodities.

In pursuance of the policy of providing bus stations at main centres, the Southern/Western National have either constructed them on their own property, or come to arrangements with local authorities to use municipally owned bus stations, at the following points since 1953:

Plymouth (Breton Side)   1958   In place of the
                                  temporary site at
                                  Union St

Paignton	1958	Jointly with Devon General Omnibus & Touring Co Ltd
Tavistock	1958	
Ilfracombe (Broad St)	1962	
Camborne	1963	
Weymouth (Edward St)	1963	
Callington (New Rd)	1963	
Minehead	1967	Reconstructed 1971
Bridgwater	1967	
Yeovil	1968	
Penzance	1968	
St Just, West Cornwall	1968	(A miniscule bus station provided by the local authority!)
St Austell	1970	Reconstruction of the company's premises and facilities in the Station Yard

By 1957, the rebuilding of the central repair and overhaul shops at Laira Bridge garage, Plymouth, had been completed and staff and equipment, temporarily moved to Bideford after the wartime bombing, gradually returned to Plymouth again.

After 30 years at 48/50 Queen Street, Exeter, which though possessing a beautiful early 19th century facade, had certain drawbacks compared with modern standards of office accommodation, Western/Southern National moved in 1961 into their new headquarters, National House, on the opposite side of the road.

From 1953 onward, it has been a story of gradually contracting services, as traffic declined with a changing social outlook and the desire for personal freedom of movement. The impact is particularly noticeable in rural areas where bus services have always been infrequent. In such cases, improvement of service is unjustifiable on financial grounds, yet there remains a minority of people who need public transport facilities. How best to cater for these is the core of the present rural transport problem. The position has been further aggravated by the declining population in many West Country rural areas, because of the progressive mechanisation of farming and the general trend of people towards the amentities of the larger towns. Busy inter urban services have by and large kept their 1953 frequencies, with judicious pruning during the evenings and on Sundays. Another post war trend which has worked adversely for bus companies is the growth of television. Whereas people previously went out for their evening's entertainment and there was a brisk late traffic on buses from cinema goers, this has largely ceased with entertainment in one's own home, and all evening bus services have had to be drastically curtailed. The same is generally true of Sunday services, where people no longer use public transport to visit the seaside and country; most either own cars, or go out in friends' or family cars at the weekend. The day is not far off when Sunday services may cease altogether except on certain key routes. On the other hand, the picture is not one of unrelieved gloom, as the post war policy of building new housing estates on the perimeter of towns, has led to a growth in town bus services.

The opening of the new Tamar Bridge in 1961, giving Plymouth direct road access to Saltash and East Cornwall, was also a development which gave an impetus to bus services. Three routes, which had previously terminated at Saltash (from Callington, Tideford and Forder) were extended across the bridge to Plymouth, the second being extended westward to Looe. Instead of the restricted traffic to Saltash, these routes were able to tap the large population reserve of Plymouth and have built up into substantial services.

Something must be said of rail closures, which have been particularly marked in the West Country since 1950, with an added impetus provided by the Beeching Report from 1963. Many people have thought that these must have provided extra traffic and revenue for the bus companies but unfortunately, so far as Western/Southern National are concerned, quite the reverse is true. Despite all that is said of them, the railway management were capable businessmen and were not intent on throwing away something which was worth having. Where substitute bus services were provided to meet rail closures, they have proved completely unremunerative, with just two exceptions. This did not matter so much while the railways were liable for the payment of a subsidy to the bus company to cover its losses, but the 1968 Transport Act freed the railways of this obligation and left the burden squarely in the lap of the National Bus Company through its subsidiaries. Overnight Western/Southern National found themselves bereft of subsidies to the tune of approximately £100,000 per annum, a grave blow on top of the general decline in passengers and revenue. The companies therefore took the only course open to them and wherever possible got rid of the heavy burden of unremunerative rail replacement services. The exceptions mentioned above are the Barnstaple-Ilfracombe branch line (closed in October 1970) and the Taunton-Minehead branch line (closed in January 1971) where the Minister of Transport, no doubt learning from past experience, had the wisdom to order a bare minimum of replacement journeys, so that the rail traffic accrued to the benefit of the existing trunk bus routes. A list of the rail closures in the West is included in Appendix D.

The main source of economy to help offset the effects of declining traffic and rapidly rising wage costs has been concentrated on the introduction of one-man operated buses. The first service to be converted to one man operation was

Southern National's Bideford-Exeter in 1957. At first there was opposition from operating staff to the new concept of single manning but patient negotiation and bonus inducements have led to a steady conversion of single deck routes until now over 85 per cent of the Company's total stage service mileage is one man operated, and the year 1980 may see the complete elimination of bus conductors.

In April 1970 with the purchase of new VRT front entrance, rear engined, Bristol double deckers, a start was made with one man double deck operation on the Plymouth-Callington route. The conversion of routes to one man, double deck operation is still continuing to the present date.

A further source of economy has stemmed from the increased size of vehicles since 1953, arising from greater permitted lengths. This has enabled duplicate buses to be dispensed with, saving both crew costs and the capital and operating costs of a second vehicle. This is why a large bus, filled to capacity at peak hours but running half empty for the rest of the day, is a more economical proposition than a smaller bus which has to be duplicated with a second vehicle and crew at peak hours—a fact not readily understood by the public at large. The Bristol Lodekka of 1953 increased seating capacity from the post war 55 to 58 and then to 70; this bus was revolutionary in design in that it had an off set transmission with low level driving shafts, enabling the centre gangway to be lower, so that the overall height of the vehicle did not exceed the traditional lowbridge type, without the inconvenient side gangway on the upper deck. A further step was taken in 1968 when, taking advantage of still greater permitted lengths, Western/Southern National took delivery of their first rear engined 53 seater single deckers, which can virtually convey the same number of passengers as the post war double decker. The mainstay of the single deck fleet in the 1950s was the Bristol LS5G model, with horizontal under floor engine mounted amidships. Western/Southern National first took delivery of vehicles of this type in December 1952 and during the ensuing five years 135 entered the fleet. Originally 45 seaters, nearly all these vehicles were subsequently converted to 41 seat one man buses, but have now been withdrawn from service with the exception of No 1701. This bus is still in regular scheduled service, but is in fact retained as a 'preserved vehicle' as a representative of this class of vehicle. Mention should be made, however, of three other LSs still in use with Western National, not as buses, but as Mobile Training Units. These are TU1, TU3 and TU6. In 1957 the LS chassis was superseded by the Bristol MW model and subsequent deliveries of single deckers were of this type up to the arrival of the RELL; the company had 38 MW5G buses and 124 MW6G coaches in its fleet some 22 of which are still in service as one-man buses. Nevertheless, on many narrow West Country roads there was still a need for a small vehicle and this was met from 1960 onward by the intake of 30 seat SUS buses and 36 seat SULs; they were 7ft 6in wide, compared with 8ft 0in for the LS and MW and 8ft 2½in for the RELL. The SUL was widely used on the lighter rural services and some 36 SULs and 1 SUS are still owned.

In 1967, to meet the need for replacements for inexpensive, light, vehicles for rural routes, the company departed from its Bristol policy and acquired 12 Bedford VAM single deckers. Further intakes of this type were rendered unnecessary in 1968 when the Bristol LH and LHS chassis became available; the company now has 248 of the latter buses and coaches.

In a declining market, the question of acquiring local operators has been of far less importance over the past 15 years. Many have gone out of business and in several instances Western/Southern National came to the aid of villages left without public transport and introduced limited

(*above*) No 2044 at St Ives has the reversed livery as applied to four Bristol FLFs in 1966. (*A O Watkins*); (*below*) Southern National RELL No 2710 was still relatively new when pictured in Weymouth Bus Station in 1968. (*A O Watkins*)

(*above*) Transferred from the Devon General fleet to Western National, but retaining its red livery, Leyland Atlantean *Sir Francis Drake* was photographed working in Falmouth. (*Western National*); (*below*) Western National owned Devon General buses in Exeter High Street during the final stages of the bus/pedestrianisation scheme. (*Western National*)

services for shopping purposes, eg Bridgwater-Spaxton in place of Waterman, and Bridgwater-Moorlynch in place of Dibble. Nevertheless, there have been one or two judicious acquisitions, where these represented obvious economic advantages to the National companies, or where the elimination of the local operator enabled services to be reorganised and unprofitable operations turned into profitable service. In the Plymouth Joint Service area, the last remaining independent operator, Heybrook Bay Motor Services, was purchased in 1959, since when Plymouth Corporation and Western National have been the sole providers of stage carriage services in the joint area. The acquisition of Lewis Motors (Falmouth) Ltd in 1965 enabled the Falmouth-Mylor route to be recast and resulted in a route which was giving a poor return to two operators, yielding a better return to one (Western National). Similarly, the purchase of Hitchens of Newlyn enabled the Penzance-Mousehole service to be reorganised on a 12min headway instead of 10-min, although one timing each hour is still taken up by an independent operator, Mr Harvey of Mousehole. In 1968, the compact and thriving little bus business of the Millbrook Steamboat and Trading Co was purchased. This operator covered the Rame peninsular on the Cornish side of the Tamar opposite Plymouth, and a complete reorganisation enabled Western National to condense its services into two routes operated from Torpoint depot. But more important from the business angle, the elimination of this operator, enabled Western National to quote for and obtain four or five remunerative school contracts serving the area. The latest acquisition was in 1974, when the excursion and tours business of Wessex Coaches Ltd at Bridport was purchased, to supplement Western National existing tours from that centre, while in 1977 Greenslades Tours Ltd transferred its tour operations at Sidmouth to Western National and in 1978 its Torbay and Plymouth activities also.

Another trend of the past 15 years has been the gradual closing of outstations, due largely to manning difficulties and the disproportionate expense of covering sickness and annual leave. Nevertheless, the outstationed crew system had much in its favour; on the same route day after day, the men knew their passengers and could adapt themselves to idiosyncracies and individual requirements. It was a form of personal service far more acceptable to the travelling public than the ever changing crew on a rota basis. Additionly, the outstationing of vehicles avoided the empty outward journey from central depot first thing in the morning and the corresponding empty return journey last thing at night, unnecessary mileage which could spell the difference between profit and loss on rural services with only four or five journeys a day. Some outstations which have disappeared in this way are The Lizard, St Just, Porthallow, Hartland, South Molton, Wiveliscombe and Milborne Port.

A reversal of this policy was proposed for 1978, in response to a request by Devon County Council to cut mileage and reduce losses being incurred on Services 91 (Salcombe-Dartmouth) and 93 (Salcombe-Plymouth). Western National was to reopen its outstation at Salcombe with two vehicles, but the scheme was eventually dropped.

One of the principal developments in express services over the past 20 years or so has been the realisation that the traffic potential has to some extent shifted from central London to the newly developing outer towns and with this in mind, a start was made in 1955 with the introduction by Royal Blue of a direct High Wycombe-Salisbury service, followed in 1956 by a joint route with Southdown Motor Services from East Grinstead to Torquay. Two years later, through working was established jointly with Eastern National from Southend-on-Sea to Bournemouth and in 1966 from Sudbury (Suffolk) to Brixham. The pattern continued in 1967 with an Ipswich-Ilfracombe service (joint with Eastern Counties and

Grey Green Coaches) and in 1968 with a Stevenage-Wey-
mouth route, a Norwich-Bournemouth service (joint with
Eastern Counties) and London-Guildford-Aldershot-Salis-
bury-Plymouth journeys. In this way, the old concept of
express routes radiating from central London, has been
modified by criss crossing lines from the new population
centres on the perimeter; it is an excellent example of adap-
tion to changing circumstances. Parallel with these developments at the London end, Royal Blue built up and extended
its facilities into Cornwall; the opening of the Tamar Bridge
in 1962 afforded the opportunity for a new Bournemouth-
Plymouth-Penzance operation and two years later a
Plymouth-Launceston-Bude service was designed to give day
return facilities to Plymouth from all parts of Cornwall by
linking coaches at Launceston.

Winter express facilities into Cornwall started in 1954,
when the Exeter-Penzance route was operated throughout
the year; it was followed in 1962 by Exeter-Newquay-
Perranporth, in 1963 by Exeter-Helston and 1968 by Exeter-
Bude. Thus the period has seen the establishment of a regular
daily network of long distance coaches from all principal
towns in Cornwall, connecting at Exeter for London, the
Midlands and the South Coast. To accommodate this
expanding traffic, the fine new coach station at Paris Street,
Exeter, was opened in 1964. The same year Royal Blue also
started to take delivery of the latest rear engined luxury
coaches, Bristol RELH6Gs. The only setback during this
period was the enforced handover of the Royal Blue London-
Bristol-Weston-super-Mare route to Bristol Omnibus Co in
1965. The experimental Plymouth-London night service
operated daily throughout the 1966 summer period and
proved so successful that it has continued each year since.

In contrast the catastrophic winter of 1962/3 brought the
West Country widespread blizzards and snow blankets as
never before, and buses and coaches were stranded at several

inaccessible points. The most spectacular incident was the rescue by helicopter of passengers from Royal Blue and Associated Motorways coaches unable to move on the Dorset Heights between Yeovil and Dorchester. Express Service developments from 1972 are dealt with in Chapter 5.

In Plymouth, the pattern since 1953 has been one of new services and extensions to growing housing estates and industrial sites on the perimeter, offset by the familiar decline in passengers. But frequent city services are easier to adapt to a declining market, by reductions of frequency and the withdrawal of evening facilities without damage to the overall network of routes. It is the country service of only three or four journeys per day which cannot be trimmed to meet hard times. In 1957 Plymouth Joint Services renumbered their routes within a simplified 1–57 range (now 1–62) and ten years later Western and Southern National were able to follow suit and end the odd position of having a service 1 in Plymouth, a Western National service 1 at Penzance and a Southern National service 1 in Yeovil. The present method of service numbering is:

1–62	Plymouth Joint Area.
70–198	South Devon and East Cornwall including Devon General services in the Paignton, Torquay and Newton Abbot areas.
201–288	Somerset excluding Yeovil.
298–383	North Devon and Devon General services in the Exmouth, Sidmouth, Tiverton and Exeter areas.
400–499	Dorset and Yeovil.
501–595	Cornwall area.
A–U	Exeter City Services.

The County Councils have carried this numbering pattern one stage further by allocating 600–699 and 870–899 to independent operators' services in Devon and 900–999 to independent operators' services in Cornwall.

From 1960, Plymouth Corporation started to take delivery of rear engined, double deck, front entrance Leyland buses and the present fleet consists of 188 of this type and 41 of the new Leyland-National single deckers. Plymouth Corporation had the distinction of being the first operator in the South West to introduce one man double deck working in 1968 and to accommodate the rapid extension of this type of operation and the use of automatic ticket machines, the fare structure throughout the Joint Services area was modified to 3d units, both adult and child (eg 'half' of 9d = 6d). With the advent of decimal currency in February 1971, the ticket machines and fare structure were re-orientated around 1p units and children's fares once again became half the adult fare with fractions of 1p counting as 1p. A further simplification took place in December 1975 with the introduction of a 'unit stage system' based on fare stages at regular 0.85 mile intervals.

There is no doubt that 1970 was a year of crisis for road passenger transport in general and Western National in particular. Ever increasing costs and declining traffic brought about an intolerable position which meant that Western National, together with many other similarly placed bus companies in the NBC, had no alternative but to invoke the provisions of the 1968 Transport Act and advise the County Councils of Cornwall, Devon, Somerset and Dorset that, unless help was forthcoming in the form of subsidies for unremunerative rural routes, there would have to be wholesale abandonment of services and closures of uneconomic depots.

This was an unhappy time for the bus industry; on the one hand the bus companies were faced with a financial crisis and on the other, the County Councils were inexperienced, and had not yet fully realised the implications of their responsibilities under the 1968 Act and were reluctant to commit public money to the completely new concept of supporting bus services. As a result, after painful and heart-searching negotiations, Western National had no alterantive other than to close down their depots at Bude, Delabole, Kingsbridge, Liskeard, Tavistock and Lynton, to reduce Chard and Bridport to the status of large out-stations and at other depots to discontinue services which had been operated for nearly 50 years. In any case right at the start of 1970 on 1 January, Western National lost its depots at Trowbridge and Chippenham which were handed over to the Bristol Omnibus Co.

It was doubly unfortunate in that, had it been possible to look ahead three or four years to the increasing involvement of County Councils in bus operation and their wider appreciation of the issues involved, there is little doubt that most of the network abandoned could have been retained, albeit at a lower level of operation.

Taking the area county by county we summarise the situation of the last few years.

Cornwall: after its initial position of almost complete lack of interest in supporting bus services and a laissez-faire attitude in allowing local operators to pick up the pieces abandoned by Western National, the County Council is now prepared to support the bus network in full at its present level and has admitted in its Transport Policies and Programmes (submitted annually to the Minister) that local operators were only able to provide approximately 25 per cent of the previous Western National network on a piecemeal basis which did not result in a cohesive pattern of services. Moreover, Western National with county support has been able to put back a number of services jettisoned in the 'dark years' of 1971-73, for example:

Service 513 Penzance-Sancreed-Grumbla   Thursday
                                                                        shopping
                                                                     service.

Service 514 Penzance-Zennor-St. Ives   Both now
Service 515 Lands End-Zennor-St. Ives   working very
successfully in
the summer
months with
open-top
double
deckers.

Service 79 Liskeard-Morval-Looe   Friday
shopping
service.

Service 75 Torpoint-Portwrinkle   Thursday
shopping
service.

Service 77 Torpoint-Whitsands   Summer only.
Service 564 Falmouth-Helford Passage
*Service 587 Truro-Coombe Creek   Tuesday
shopping bus

*Service 596 Truro-Point   ,,
*Service 585 Truro-Idless   ,,

In addition, some new services have been started up on
County Council initiative:

Service 548 Camborne-Tehidy   Tuesdays, Thursdays,
Saturdays

*Service 597 Truro-Comford   Thursday shopping
service.

*Service 598 Truro-Stithians   Monday and Wednes-
day shopping service.

*Service 599 Truro-Mylor   Friday shopping service

*These six services form an integrated pattern of shopping
services from Truro involving one bus going to a different
destination each day, and have progressed from a tentative
experiment to a permanent feature.

The company has still been unable to regain a footing into

the large abandoned areas of North Cornwall and only the future can tell what may happen here.

Devon: this county has from the beginning shown a lively interest in bus operations and had the distinction of appointing the first Transport Co-ordinating Officer in the country. A very similar pattern has arisen to that applicable in Cornwall, although Devon has shown more interest in innovation and experimenting with new ideas. Subject to justifiable economies, the Western National current network in the county is now maintained and, as in Cornwall, Western National has been able to replace a number of services abandoned in the 1971–73 period, for example:

Service 99 Plymouth-Bigbury-on-Sea.	Weds & Suns in Summer.
Service 165 Totnes-Rattery-South Brent	Friday shopping service.
Service 318 Bideford-Bradworthy	Shopping service
Service 338 Sidmouth-Honiton	Summer service
Service 345 Tiverton-Taunton	Friday shopping service.

New services have been commenced:

Service 116 Paignton-Barton Pines Aircraft Museum	Summer service
Service 137 Torquay-Dawlish Warren	Summer service with open top double deckers.

Service 167 Extension through to Dartmouth from Cornworthy on Fris.

Service 299 Barnstaple Town Service.
Service 329 Barnstaple School Service.
Service 337 Sidmouth Town Service.
Service 343 Tiverton Town Service.
Service 365 Exeter-Moretonhampstead via Drewsteignton.

There are several other interesting developments in Devon which merit separate mention:

Dartmoor National Park: in summer 1976 a special network of services was established at weekends during the summer to cater for visitors to Dartmoor. This involves Western National and A. P. Jack, the local operator at Widecombe-in-the-Moor. Under the arrangement, Western National provides a trunk double-deck route from Plymouth to Moretonhampstead right across the heart of Dartmoor (Service 82) with special feeder journeys to Moretonhampstead from Exeter and Newton Abbot on existing services 359 and 173. Jack provides minibus services between Widecombe—Bovey Tracey and Buckfastleigh—Postbridge. The experiment proved successful, particularly Service 82, and the network is now a regular summer feature, Wednesdays having been added as an additional day of operation in July and August.

Exmoor National Park: following the pattern established on Dartmoor, the County Council in conjunction with the National Park Authority has revitalised existing Western National Service 306 Ilfracombe—Lynton and introduced a new Service 320 Barnstaple—Hunters Inn, the two services connecting at Easterclose with through fare facilities to Hunters Inn from Ilfracombe and Lynton. Both services are operated on a daily basis during the summer months, and the introduction of an Exmoor Rambler Ticket (two adults and two children) has ensured the success of the experiment.

Midi-Bus Schemes: the County Council has shown great interest in sponsoring the operation of small 27-seater buses in situations which call for vehicles of smaller dimensions than usual. Three services employing such vehicles are now in operation:-

Service 119   Brixham Town Service, using narrow estate roads; this vehicle also interworks existing Service 112 Paignton—Greenway where small buses are required.

Service H   Exeter Bus Station-Royal Devon & Exeter Hospital complex enabling the vehicle to proceed into the hospital grounds to a point adjacent to the main entrance.

Service N   Exeter High Street-Winslade Park, to cater for new office complex.

Devon County Council has also taken an active part in helping to redesign and implement large-scale reorganisations of existing services on an area basis, enabling economies to be effected and the rejuvenation of remote unremunerative rural routes by the extension or diversion of trunk services. Such schemes have been carried out in the Crediton area and the Tiverton/Cullompton area.

Since 1978 the County Council has taken the line that bus subsidies should best be directed to supporting and promoting rural transport and it advised Western National that no grants would henceforth be made towards urban networks in Exeter and Torbay, since they could be rendered economic by sensible reductions in frequency and reorganisations. Accordingly Western National introduced schemes in both these town areas in February 1978 designed to place the services on a self-supporting basis.

With the help of the County Council an overall sort-out of facilities was effected with Messrs Lovering, a local coach operator in Ilfracombe, enabling his two small stage services to be discontinued and integrated with existing Western National routes, in exchange for certain concessions on Tours from Ilfracombe. This settlement also ensured that Messrs Lovering would not object to the new Exmoor National Park stage services mentioned above.

In the eastern part of Western National territory County support can be summarised as follows:

Dorset: this county has not been so active as Devon and Cornwall in the promotion of bus services but has nevertheless ensured the continuation of the Western National network in Dorset subject to reasonable economies. The routes operated in the county have tended to remain static since 1972. With additional school contract work at Bridport, this outstation has built up almost to its previous depot strength and certain engineering facilities have been restored.

Somerset: this county has not supplied the full level of funds necessary to maintain the Western National network of bus services in its area with the result that the story at Taunton, Yeovil, Minehead and Bridgwater depots has been one of progressive depletion of bus facilities. Bridgwater and Minehead depots have been reduced to the status of large outstations. In some respects it is sad that the implementation of government policy on public transport has been left to the interpretation of county councils who may be swayed by political or short-term consideration of a very local nature. Yet it must be recorded that the Council was not slow in buying the track bed of the Taunton-Minehead railway and leasing it to the privately-run West Somerset Railway Company.

In the matter of timetable presentation, Cornwall and Devon County Councils have also shown a lively and progressive interest and the Western National timetable books have been expanded into comprehensive public transport documents containing details of bus, coach, rail, air and ferry services within the counties. This has undoubtedly been of great assistance to the public, both resident and visitors, who can now find all they require in the matter of transport facilities within one timetable book.

The 1968 Transport Act also enabled all local authorities (county, district and parish councils) to provide concessionary fares for old age pensioners, blind and disabled persons, recognising that this was an item which should more properly be borne by the community as a whole through rates levied, than by bus companies, whose financial stringencies could only enable them to reduce fares for one section of the travelling public at the expense of the remainder. The South West is placed in a very difficult situation in this respect, in view of the large numbers of retired people who come to live in the area, so that any concessionary fare scheme for pensioners is bound to have a disproportionately large financial cost. Nevertheless, a number of district and parish councils throughout the four western counties have seen fit to introduce special fare schemes by way of half-fare passes, vouchers or tokens, in each case the bus company being reimbursed by the council to the value of the normal fare for the journey taken. The only drawback arises from the fact that some local authorities have adopted concessionary fare schemes and some have not, which means that people living within short distances of each other receive different treatment, for example pensioners residing within Exeter City receive concessions but those in the surrounding rural areas only two to three miles from the city centre do not; as usual the bus company tends to receive the blame for this! Much has been said about reduced fares being able to generate more passengers for bus companies and to test this theory Western National, with the backing of Cornwall and Devon County Councils carried out a number of reduced fare experiments in 1976/7. The results were quite conclusive; in all cases there was an increase in passengers but not sufficient to compensate for the lower fares charged. In North Devon, for example a 33⅓ per cent reduction in fares produced 15 per cent more passengers but 18 per cent reduction in revenue. Similar results have been obtained by other bus companies throughout the country but despite this, there is no lack of well-meaning folk losing no opportunity in council chambers and the media to tell the bus companies how to make more money by reducing fares. But then everyone knows that everyone knows how to run buses except professional busmen. Clearly there is no easy way of inducing people to use public transport and if the British bus system is to be maintained in anything like its present shape there must be close co-operation with local authorities in overall transport planning—even possibly curbs on private cars in town or city centres.

A development which has been an unqualified success in recent years has been the introduction of open-top buses on scenic routes during the summer months. No holiday-maker can resist the appeal of a summer's day ride on the wind-blown upper deck—perhaps it is the sailor who is said to reside in every British heart. For many years, Devon General had open-toppers on seaside routes within the Torbay urban complex and Western National had one around the beaches and headland at Falmouth. But the last three years have seen bold experiments with open-toppers on long coastal services with running times of one hour or more. The buses themselves have a roof and windows for the top deck which is removed for the summer but put back in position for winter operation. The most spectacular experiment was the introduction of these vehicles on the St Ives—Lands End service in Summer 1977, one of the wildest and most scenic coast roads in Britain, including a hair-raising descent into Sennen Cove. The service, which had just ticked along during July and August only in previous years with single-deckers, was doubled in frequency, ran through from June to September and quadrupled its earnings per mile. Western National accordingly took delivery of a batch of new open-toppers in 1978. Like the earlier Torbay open toppers they carry names of naval personalities or famous ships of the Royal Navy. Indeed some of the Devon General open toppers carry the names of Devon sea dogs reviving the names carried on the first Devon General double deckers of 1919. The routes now in operation with this type of bus in the Summer months are:

122	Babbacombe	—Paignton Zoo
123	,,	—Kingswear
124	,,	—Brixham
137	Torquay	—Dawlish Warren
412	Weymouth	—Bridport via Abbotsbury
514	Penzance	—Zennor—St Ives
515	St Ives	—Lands End
569	Falmouth	—Pendennis Head
570	Newquay	—St Columb Minor

Another very sensible and useful innovation in vehicle type during recent years has been the dual-purpose single-decker. This is not only suitable for operation as a one-man operated bus, but its coach type seats and smart appearance make it suitable for use on excursions and tours, private hire work and long-distance express services. These buses are performing stalwart service on long-distance bus routes and have solved the long-standing problem of the separate, expensive coach fleet as distinct from the bus fleet.

A revolutionary idea, as yet in its infancy, is the concept of the park and ride service. This is of particular relevance in the South-West with its unspoiled resorts with quaint narrow streets, which were becoming completely spoiled and congested with the pressure of private car traffic. The park and ride concept envisages the establishment of car parks on the perimeter of vulnerable areas, with a car-parking fee which includes a shuttle bus trip to and from the town centre. A scheme at Dartmouth (whose peculiar geographical location precludes the construction of large car parks within the town) was a huge success in 1977 and the two small initial single-deck buses had to be replaced by double-deckers in the peak of the season. An experiment on similar lines at Falmouth in 1977 was not successful (owing to injudicious routing) but an amendment during summer 1978 rendered the service as successful as the Dartmouth scheme and double deckers will be used in 1979. Another scheme started in 1978 served Brixham from Churston, and Barnstaple and Truro are to have park and ride schemes in 1979. With increasing urban congestion and the increasing cost of providing town-centre car parks, the park and ride concept is here to stay.

Bus priorities are also a development of the future, the most outstanding example in Western National territory being the pedestrianisation of High Street, Exeter, with access for city bus services only. This has transformed the City Centre from a busy noisy thoroughfare, to a spacious tree-planted area where shoppers can spread out and go about their business in comparative peace although still enjoying the facility of an on-the-spot bus service. Minor buses only schemes are also in operation in Newton Abbot, Torquay and Bridgwater, which obviate buses making lengthy one-way detours enforced upon other traffic.

A recent innovation (1977) involving co-operation in its widest sense, is the Exe Valley Market Bus scheme, serving an area of small, remote villages north-west of Tiverton. This is a region where there is insufficient potential to support conventional bus services and the two Western National routes (Tiverton-Rackenford and Tiverton-Stoodleigh) had reached a point where withdrawal seemed inevitable. Under the sponsorship of Devon County Council, a mini bus was supplied by the Department of Environment (Transport Research Laboratory) and a blanket licence covering an area of several parishes was obtained by Western National, enabling facilities to be provided from any point to and from Tiverton. But the principle innovation was in the manning of the bus, which was undertaken by volunteer drivers from among residents of the villages concerned. Western National undertook the training of the drivers and is also responsible for the mechanical maintenance of the bus. The villages concerned formed a special bus committee to administer the scheme, arrange the routing of the bus and deal with the finances. Intending passengers phone the committee in advance, state their boarding point and the bus is routed so as to pick up all these passengers. The scheme got off to a very good and enthusiastic start and there was no lack of volunteer drivers. It gives every promise of becoming firmly established and is on the way to becoming self-supporting financially.

After the gloom and pessimism of the early 1970s, it is a pleasure to end this chapter on a note of optimism, with the bus well on the way to becoming accepted as fulfilling a vital social role and with government and local authorities exercising vital powers to ensure that public transport continues to be available, even in the smallest of villages.

(*above*) Bristol LHS at Mousehole. (Western National); (*below*) Bristol VR and A P Jacks' Ford Transit on the special Dartmoor services in 1977. (*Western National*)

(*above*) One of the Ford/Alexander midi buses on the recently introduced service at Brixham. (*Western National*); (*below*) decorated for the Queen's Silver Jubilee is Western National Bristol VR LOD 724P, and behind it a Plymouth City Transport, Leyland Atlantean. (*Western National*)

4 Devon General Omnibus and Touring Co Ltd

The story of the Devon General Omnibus and Touring Co Ltd has two sources, based on the towns of Exeter and Torquay. There could be no greater contrast: Exeter is a city as ancient as any in Great Britain with roots going back into the twilight days well before the coming of the Romans; Torquay is a modern resort which has grown up in the last 200 years around the tiny fishing villages in Torbay.

It was in Exeter on 22 May 1919 that the company was founded, to take over from John Stuart Mill three AEC B-type, open top double deckers, named Drake, Raleigh, and Hawkins after the famous Elizabethan seamen associated with South Devon. The registered offices were in Forest Hill, London, and John Stuart Mill became the first chairman. At the same time a few single deckers, char-a-bancs and lorry buses were purchased, all on reconditioned army lorry chassis. The objective of the newly-formed company, in addition to serving the immediate catchment area of Exeter, was to link Exeter with Newton Abbot and Torquay and to commence bus services within the latter two places. The first three services started in July 1919 and within twelve months of its inception the company had established regular services on the following routes:

1   Exeter-Dawlish-Teignmouth-Newton Abbot-
     Torquay
2   Exeter-Chudleigh-Newton Abbot-Torquay
3   Exeter-Newton Abbot-Ashburton-Buckfastleigh

3A   Torquay-Newton Abbot-Ashburton-Buckfastleigh
4   Torquay-Maidencombe-Shaldon
5   Exeter-Clyst St Mary-Woodbury-Exmouth-Budleigh
     Salterton

Concurrently with the bus services, Devon General built up a service for the collection and delivery of parcels and goods, the lighter merchandise being carried on luggage canopies on the buses, while heavy goods were delivered by lorry. Delivery of goods was undertaken on the day consigned, anywhere within a 25 mile radius of Exeter. A garage was erected in Exeter in 1920 and two others followed at Kingsteignton and Exmouth.

Bodies for the company's first char-a-bancs were constructed by a local Exeter firm, Messrs A. G. Dowell of Russell Street and the livery for all vehicles was LGOC red with white lines, chassis black, wheels brown, and Devon General in gold lettering on the sides.

Meanwhile in Torquay the National Electric Construction Co formed a subsidiary, the Torquay Tramways Co Ltd, in August 1904, to implement the powers obtained by the parent company for a system of electric tramways in the Borough. The first three routes, laid to a track gauge of 3ft 6in were:

Beacon Quay to Torre Station via Strand and Castle Circus
Strand to St Marychurch via Ellacombe
Torre Station to St Marychurch via Upton

Rolling stock consisted of 18 four wheel, open top, cars with Brush bodies, seating 22 inside and 27 outside, mounted on Mountain and Gibson, 8ft 6in wheel base, radial trucks. They were typical, spartan turn of the century tramcars, but nothing could be wholly commonplace in so select a town as

126

Torquay, where there was strong public feeling against the erection of poles and overhead wiring. The Dolter system of current collection was therefore used, the electricity supply being taken from the corporation power station at Upton Vale through the tramway depot and workshops located near the St Marychurch terminus.

This extraordinary and now wholly extinct method of propulsion, can briefly be described as a form of electrical leap frog. The tram was equipped with a long collector shoe or magnetic skate, just above the road surface, which made contact with a series of metal studs set centrally in the roadway between the rails. The studs were connected with a continuous electric cable below the road and the pressure of the skate on the studs energised them in turn and the tram was drawn along magnetically. The system proved costly and wasteful of current, besides being a danger to other traffic, not to mention the hazards to human and animal life. The following description of a tramcar powered by this method (not at Torquay in this particular instance) makes hair raising reading:

As we passed over the connectional studs, we seemed at times to be travelling over sheets of fire, the electric flashes ever and anon blazing from beneath the wheel with startling vividness, caused I believe by skidding over the studs and not finding contact evenly . . . With the flash came a swishing sound similar to the send-off of a burning rocket. The lights in the car too, danced in and out with frivolous frequency. Altogether the effects on a night journey lent a spice of variety to the run.

Trams also tended to get stuck between studs!

In November 1907 a road widening scheme enabled the Strand-St Marychurch route to be operated on a circular basis via Ellacombe and Wellswood and in the following

April the route was extended to Torquay railway station. The tramway company next reached agreement with Paignton Urban District Council, for an extension of the tramway to Paignton railway station. Until the recent formation of the all inclusive Borough of Torbay, there was always a certain amount of rivalry between Paignton and Torquay, and Paignton Council insisted (perhaps not surprisingly) on overhead current collection! This placed the company in a difficult position but no doubt due to the unsatisfactory nature of the Dolter system, it was able to persuade Torquay Corporation to agree to overhead wiring. As a result the two towns were linked by tram in July 1911, replacing the open top bus service operated by the Great Western Railway. At this time, 15 additional tramcars were purchased to meet the needs of the extended network, and to house the growing fleet an additional depot with four tracks was built at Preston on the outskirst of Paignton.

So far as the Torquay Tramways was concerned, the years 1912–1918 were uneventful and World War I did not affect its operations. The Company, however, was alive to the rapid post-war development of motor transport and in 1919 announced its proposal to initiate regular motor bus services on inter-urban routes embracing Newton Abbot, Teignmouth, Dawlish, Exeter and Torquay. The first route started in May 1920 between Torre and Newton Abbot, followed shortly after by Newton Abbot-Dawlish. This new field of activities brought the tramway company into direct and intense competition with the Devon General Company, which itself had been expanding rapidly during 1921 under the able and progressive chairmanship of Mr Walter Flexman French, who played so large a part in the development of bus transport in Southern England.

The conflict was resolved in June 1922 by the tramway company purchasing Devon General and reconstituting the board of directors; Mr French departed, to look after his other bus interests further eastward. Two months later the tramway company's motor buses were transferred to the new Devon General Company, giving a combined fleet of 42 buses and 13 char-a-bancs; services were completely revised, to avoid competition with the tramway system and to combat competition from other sources. The new bus fleet was garaged at the tramway depot in Westhill Avenue, Torquay. Devon General was thus established as the predominant bus operator in the area, which it continued to serve for over 50 years.

In 1923 the newly formed bus company issued its first timetable booklet of 64 pages for 1d. It is interesting to note that the Exeter-Exmouth journey took 70min at this time, compared with the average of 47min now. Although running times have improved over the past 50 years certain other facilities have not, for we find among the 1923 regulations and conditions that bicycles were carried at owners risk and charged for at the rate of 1s (5p) if accompanied by a fare-paying passenger or 2s (10p) otherwise; also that perambulators would only be carried at owners risk on the roof of the bus if the wheels were dismantled!

In these early years, Devon General recognised that to maintain its position of ascendancy, expansion and the purchase of other operators was essential. The first significant acquisition took place in March 1924, when the company strengthened its hold on the territory east and north of Exeter by the purchase of Croscols of Tiverton. This company was a subsidiary of Crosville Motor Services and Colwills of Ilfracombe, which had started activities on 5 April 1921 with a bus service from Tiverton to Dulverton via Bampton. This was followed on 6 May by a Tiverton-Exeter service and subsequently by a Tiverton-Cullompton/Uffculme route. Devon General contested this development by introducing an Uffculme-Cullompton-Exeter service. Thereafter Crosville, recognising the difficulty of controlling activities so remote from their head office in Chester, sold Croscols to Devon General.

In the same year there was another significant acquisition, this time in the sphere of coach tour operations, when the business of Fleet Cars Ltd was bought. This had been founded in 1919 by Captain Hutt to operate char-a-bancs from Torquay and Paignton and at the time of purchase by Devon General the fleet consisted of five yellow Dennis vehicles. The value of an established trading name was recognised by Devon General and the name Fleet Cars was retained. A garage was acquired in Orient Road, Paignton, to house the 21 new Lancia coaches purchased between 1925 and 1927 to replace the original five and to develop the coach tours business.

Devon General obviously realised early in its history the value of diversifying its business, supplementing the ordinary bus services with coach tours. To this end it further strengthened its position in Paignton by the purchase of Comfy Coaches in 1925 and White Heather tours in 1927.

During 1926 two further significant developments occurred, first the agreement with Devon Motor Transport described in Chapter 2 and second the purchase of the Ashburton-Torquay service of E. O. Babington; this operator had established himself at the expense of Devon General by running more attractive vehicles.

In 1927 a very interesting acquisition took place, that of the Torquay and Chelston Steam Car Co Ltd whose antecedents went back before Devon General or the Torquay trams and could probably claim to have originated public passenger transport in the Torbay area. The company traced its origins to the Torquay & District Motor Omnibus Co Ltd which commenced operations in 1903 with Clarkson steam buses. Between 1903 and 1905 eight of these vehicles, painted red and cream, were put into service and gave good account of themselves on the hilly routes on which they operated. Some people hoped that the steam buses would forestall tramways in Torquay but they were disappointed and the business ceased in 1907, the steam buses being sold to the newly formed Harrogate Road Car Company (now West Yorkshire Road Car Co Ltd). Local support for the steam buses was still strong, however, and in the same year the Torquay Road Car Co Ltd was formed with two Clarkson steam buses acquired from the Vale of Llangollen Co and others purchased from the Eastbourne Omnibus Co. These steamers pioneered the bus service over the 36 mile route between Torquay and Plymouth via Totnes, South Brent and Ivybridge. Unfortunately, the Torquay Road Car Co Ltd ceased operating in 1911 to be succeeded in the following year by the Torquay & Chelston Company. About the same time, three local tradesmen in Newton Abbot organised a steam bus service to Kingsteignton, but went bankrupt after three months and sold their two Clarkson steamers to the Harrogate Road Car Co for £37.

In all matters, it is the clear sighted, adaptable and enterprising who survive and Devon General management demonstrated these qualities. In the summer of 1928, realising the potential of bus travel over longer distances, the company inauguarated limited stop services jointly with the National Omnibus and Transport Co Ltd under the name of Devon National Amalgamated Services:

> Exeter—Plymouth (still operating)
> Exeter—Ilfracombe (ceased 1939)
> Torquay—Plymouth (still operating)
> Torquay—Exeter—Lyme Regis

The Torquay-Exeter service is still in operation but the Exeter-Lyme Regis section was incorporated in the Exeter-Weymouth stage service (jointly operated with Western National) which ceased as a through facility on 21 February

1971. Between 1957 and 1959 the Exeter-Torquay limited stop service was extended experimentally to Paignton but proved unsuccessful. Two other services were:

Torquay-Taunton (this service was withdrawn after six months)
Exeter-Minehead

The latter was a limited stop operation and ceased in 1935 but a through connecting stage service with Western National is still running. Since 1963 a Royal Blue express service (now National Travel) has operated on summer Saturdays between Plymouth, Exeter and Minehead, principally to cater for Butlins Camp, Minehead.

During the period 1928–1933 Devon General embarked on a comprehensive vehicle renewal programme under which the old fleet was replaced by new Leylands. In 1930 and 1931 agreement was reached with Exeter Corporation for the construction of a bus station in Paul Street and depots were set up at Sidmouth, Exeter and Moretonhampstead. But the most important building development of 1931 was the completion of the large garage, workshops and head offices at Newton Road, Torquay, replacing the premises at Westhill Avenue which had become inadequate. The Newton Road garage has accommodation for 140 vehicles and the head office administration of the Company continued from these premises until 1 January 1970. But the most far-reaching event of 1931 was the acquisition of the National Electric Construction Co Ltd (of which Devon General was still a subsidiary) by the British Electric Traction Co.

There was also a group of small operators who started up on the Paignton-Brixham road during the 1920s:

J. Mills (Bluebird), Brixham
Prout, Churston.

132

J. Low, Paignton.
H. Cooper (Dandy Cars), Paignton.
Soul and Sanders (Paigntonian), Paignton.
J. Geddes (Burton Cars), Brixham.

They had proved troublesome to Devon General and in 1931 they were bought out and their vehicles disposed of, although Devon General continued to use one of their garages at Churston for a time. For one of the six—Mr Geddes of the Burton Hotel—this was not the end of the road. He commenced in April 1925 with a second hand canvas-covered maroon-painted Fiat and operated all the year round between Brixham and Kingswear plus a summer only service between Brixham and Paignton. Although the latter service was purchased by Devon General in 1931, a joint agreement was reached in respect of the Brixham-Kingswear route which continues on this basis to the present day. Mr Geddes's son Mr Bruce Geddes is one of the few remaining local operators within Devon General territory and in fact he extended his activities in 1950 by the introduction of a new service between Brixham and Sharkham Point (holiday caravan site). In 1976 the company (which also operates local excursions and tours and private hire) was renamed Brixham Coaches Ltd.

In 1932 Devon General made another important acquisition in the coach tour business when it purchased Grey Cars from A. Timpson and Sons Ltd of Catford, London, including the two-level garage at Torwood Street, Torquay, which was in use until 1978 as a coach garage. It was transferred to Western National ownership and subsequently to Greenslades, but when its Torquay operations reverted to Devon General, Torwood St garage was put up for sale. Grey Cars originated in 1913 when the South Devon Garages and Motor Touring Co Ltd took over two coaches from Messrs Grists of Torquay, added extra vehicles to the

fleet and operated tours under the title The Grey Torpedo
Cars. This rather frightening name, at a time when motor
vehicles were in their infancy and still liable to go off bang
at any time, was quickly modified by the omission of Torpedo;
after World War 1 the fleet expanded rapidly by the addition
of AEC and Daimler char-a-bancs. In 1921 18 vehicles were
owned and it was in this year that the Grey Cars emblem
appeared, together with the first pneumatic tyred vehicle.
The company was also reconstituted as The Grey Cars Ltd
and in 1928 Timpson's purchased the business and built the
Torwood Street garage; the fleet name was retained.

In 1934 Devon General decided to wind up its two subsidiaries Fleet Cars and Grey Cars although the fleetname
and livery of the latter were retained until 1936 when the
coaches received the Devon General fleetname although
retaining grey livery. Finally in 1939 most of the Devon
General coach fleet was repainted saxe blue, but as will be
seen later in this chapter, Grey Cars had a surprising
resurrection in post war years. Between 1934 and 1940 Devon
General purchased a number of businesses (see Appendix C)
which, among other things, strengthened their position in
Sidmouth, Teignmouth and Exmouth.

The road motor services of the railway companies im-
pinged on Devon General territory at two points—Paignton
and Bovey Tracey/Moretonhampstead/Chagford. At Paignton
the GWR started routes to Totnes on 20 April 1905, and in
1926 to Greenway on the River Dart. With a countrywide
publicity scheme sponsored by Torquay and Paignton
councils and boosted by the GWR at its principal stations,
the Torbay area was promoted as an attractive seaside
resort. The resultant influx of holiday makers did much to
boost the development of public road transport both by bus
and tram.

With the formation of Western National and the reorganisation of services in 1930, local routes from Paignton

were divided between Devon General and Western National, the latter company taking over all the GWR vehicles at Paignton and placing them under the supervision of Totnes depot.

The GWR inaugurated three feeder bus services to its Newton Abbot-Moretonhampstead branch line:

(i) Bovey Tracey-Haytor-Widecombe-in-the-Moor, September 1924

(ii) Bovey Tracy-Becky Falls-Manaton, September 1925,

(iii) Moretonhampstead-Chagford.

Feeders (i) and (ii) both succeeded services commenced by Bovey Tours on 22 May 1922. In 1929 this group of routes passed to Western National but were transferred to Devon General in 1934. The Exeter-Moretonhampstead-Chagford route is still operated by Devon General but the two moorland routes from Bovey Tracey were withdrawn some 20 years ago. Since 1976, however, under the sponsorship of Devon County Council, the Dartmoor network of services has achieved a new lease of life (see Chapter 3).

During the early 1920s Torquay Corporation constructed a cliff railway connecting Oddicombe Beach with the main road at Babbacombe Downs, a distance of $\frac{1}{2}$ mile, with a gradient of 1 in 2.84. It was opened on 1 April 1926 and running rights were leased to Torquay Tramways, which painted the two cars in tramway livery. With the cessation of tramway operation the cliff railway reverted to the Corporation; the original cars lasted until 1964 and the replacements, in Corporation colours, are still working today. By the early 1930s, in common with many other tramway systems, the Torquay trams were in a run down state and in need of replacement. An agreement was reached in 1933 with Torquay Corporation and Paignton UDC about the future of the tramways; the two local authorities waived their right of purchase and agreed to the replacement of trams with motor buses, in spite of a strong local campaign for trolley-buses. The die was cast and on 14 January 1934 the Torquay-Paignton trams ceased, followed on 31 January by the remaining three routes. For replacements, 24 AEC Regent double deck buses with 52 seat highbridge bodies by Short Bros were purchased. The trams were scrapped, with the exception of six bogie cars and six four-wheel double deck cars sold to Plymouth Corporation. The overhead equipment was dismantled and the rails gradually taken up, but the poles along the main roads and sea front were given a face lift and some remain in use for street lighting! Westhill Avenue depot passed to Torquay Corporation, and Preston depot was sold to a firm of motor engineers.

There was one other small development before the dark shadow of World War II overtook bus operators. This was the establishment in 1937 of a Coastal Cruise service, traversing the scenic Marine Drive at Torquay; it was operated by two Bedford vehicles in saxe-blue livery with unglazed side windows. The service had a very short life, being withdrawn on the outbreak of war and never resumed.

On the outbreak of war in 1939, the military authorities requisitioned a large number of the company's single deck vehicles, no doubt on the assumption that an operator in a predominately holiday area would not need the buses in wartime. However the process appears to have gone too far and in 1940 Devon General had to borrow five Leyland Titan double deckers from Southdown Motor Services and again in 1942 two ex Tilling AEC Regents with outside stairs from London Transport. By 1943 the wartime utility buses had begun to trickle through and all the loaned vehicles were sent home again. Torwood Street garage at Torquay was taken over by the RAF for the duration of the war and although the company's coach fleet was used on special workmen's services, the majority of vehicles were put in store at Court Garage, Torquay, and at Moretonhampstead and Sidmouth depots. For a while several AEC Regents at Torquay ran on producer gas but the Devon General effort in this respect does not compare with the extensive producer gas operations carried out by the Western/Southern National.

By the end of the war, although it had suffered no great loss of vehicles through enemy action, Devon General found that the majority of its vehicles needed major repairs, and an extensive rehabilitation programme was put in hand. Three coaches were reconditioned and were able to carry out a greatly reduced tours programme at Torquay in 1945. As the coaches were, in effect, starting up afresh, the opportunity was taken to revive the old popular Grey Cars fleet name. The experiment seemed to meet with public approval and in the following season, 1946, the entire coach fleet emerged in Grey Cars livery, first at Torquay and subsequently at Exeter, Exmouth, Tiverton and Newton Abbot.

Wars and catastrophes have their place in the scheme of things; they serve as spurs to human effort and direct ingenuity and resourcefulness into fresh channels. World War I hastened the perfection of the internal combustion engine and other mechanical devices and ushered in a period of individualism and competition; World War II caused a swing in a new direction and taught the social interdependence of human beings—the emphasis shifted from individualism to co-operation. The established virtues of the 1920s and 1930s became the vices of the 1960s and 1970s (and very much vice versa!). In the South West, the trend towards voluntary coordination in transport began in Plymouth in 1942 with the Joint Services Scheme between the Plymouth Corporation and Western National described in Chapter 3. Exeter was not far behind and in 1947 the Exeter Joint Agreement between the City Transport Department and Devon General was concluded, for reasons broadly similar to those at Plymouth. Under the Exeter coordination scheme, each partner agreed to operate equal mileage in an area within a ten mile radius from the centre of the city. Fare restrictions were swept away and there was an unrestricted interchange of vehicles within the Joint Area, Corporation buses being seen on rural routes and Devon General buses on Exeter City services. Exeter, with a current population of approximately 100,000 is the main commercial and shopping centre for a very wide catchment area and the joint service scheme did much to promote an efficient public transport system within this area, employing vehicles and resources to the maximum advantage.

The Exeter Joint scheme linked the fortunes of the City Transport Department with those of Devon General. It was in 1882 that the Exeter Tramways Co Ltd opened three short routes worked by horse drawn trams. Local opposition to the laying of tram rails in main streets led to alternative and less attractive routes being found, with the result that passenger traffic was light and the system almost fell into disuse. This is an interesting example of the failure of local traders to appreciate that, far from discouraging trade, an efficient public transport system routed through the main thorough-fares is a great asset; it is a lesson which is only just being learned to the full. However, Exeter Corporation stepped in and saved the situation by purchasing the Tramway Company in 1903 and immediately set about revising the routes and extending and electrifying the whole system. The first two electric tram routes were opened on 4 April 1905 from the Guildhall via High Street to Midway Terrace, Heavitree and from St David's station via High Street to Pinhoe Road (Abbey Road). The original fleet consisted of 14 four wheel open top trams, with conventional overhead wiring; current was supplied from the Corporation's own power station. By 1906 the network was complete with extensions from Heavitree terminus by Midway Terrace to

Cross Park, and tracks were laid down Fore Street Hill and and across Exe Bridge to terminals at Alphington Road (Waterloo Road) and Cowick Street (Dunsford Road); in contrast, the St Davids station section was curtailed at Queen Street (Clock Tower). The fleet was supplemented over the years with additional four wheel open top cars, the last four being delivered new in 1929. The maximum tram fleet was 32 vehicles.

In 1929 Exeter Corporation decided on the inevitable change to buses and before the end of that year, seven single deck buses were working on new routes to the suburbs. Bus operation in the Exeter suburbs was no new thing, for Devon General had previously operated a Topsham Road-Bedford Circus service with solid tyred, front entrance, vehicles and even before this had experimented with a Mount Radford Inn-Magdalen Street-South Street route, which was withdrawn because of a lack of passengers. In 1930 six AEC Regent double deck buses replaced the trams on the Pinhoe Road-Alphington Road route. The replacement process continued until, by the end of July 1931, trams only ran between Heavitree and the depot at the foot of Paris Street. The ceremonial closure took place on 19 August 1931, when Mr E. C. Perry drove No. 14 to the depot; as Mayor of Exeter, he had driven the inaugural car in 1905. Several trams were sold for futher service in Halifax and Plymouth, the remainder being scrapped.

So ended a comparatively short lived and uneventful tramway system, enlivened by one dramatic incident on 7 March 1917, when car No 12 ran away down Fore Street hill and finally left the rails and overturned on Exe Bridge, killing one passenger and a horse in its headlong career. In these days, a road accident involving a death is no great news, but in 1917 the runaway tramcar made the main headlines and occupied half the front page of the *Express and Echo*. The press report is a gem of its period, beginning soberly and objectively but soon warming to its theme with eye witness accounts and personal experiences with a high pitch of drama:

> Great excitement was caused in Exeter this morning when it was learned that owing to an apparently runaway tramcar, accidents had occurred on Fore Street hill and at Exe Bridge, with fatal results. The casualities included one woman—a passenger on the car—killed and several injured. A waggon horse was also killed . . . Mr Herbert Chant, a well known local comedian, who performs under the name of Burt, saw the whole of the car's journey down Fore Street hill: 'The driver of the tram, as he passed me, was doing all he could to get the brakes to work. After he struck the van (this was when the horse was killed) I think he realised his case was pretty well hopeless and I shall not easily forget the expression on his face. Women were in the car and they were crying out. The car gained momentum and was soon *flying* down the hill: it must have attained a speed of at least 30 *miles an hour*. I and several others ran down Fore Street shouting at the top of our voices . . .'

As the tram approached Exe Bridge, the story is elaborated by a lad of 15 employed as a brass cleaner at the tram depot who was actually on the car:

> At the points near Mr Footes greengrocers shop, an upward car from St Thomas was waiting to pass. It looked as if the runaway car would have smashed into it but it went off on its own pair of rails . . .

An elderly lady exclaimed 'I am saved! Saved by chance! I was going to get on the car and then decided to walk.' The conductress was taken into the boot repairing depot of Mr George May who said:

(*above*) Inspector Rickard supervises the first departure to Bournemouth after World War II on 15 April 1946. (*Collection of A E Rickard*); (*below*) the earliest ECW bodied LS coaches had four bay construction. No 1740 was ordered in 1952 and compares with the long-lived subsequent design sported by No 1365 in this 1965 view of Southern National coaches at Barnstaple. (*A O Watkins*)

No 324 is one of the Plaxton bodied Bristol LH6Ls specially built for Green-slades to a width of 7ft 6in for operation on Dartmoor and Exmoor. (*Collection of Greenslades*)

The conductress of the car came along at that moment and almost fell into my arms. I took her at once into my shop. She cried out—'Oh dear, oh dear, my car has run away! look, look!' Then she went on to say that an elderly lady passenger had pushed her off as she was standing on the back platform. She seemed very anxious about the passengers and all her thought was for them and her tram money which she seemed to think she had lost in falling off.

After its headlong negotiation of the points at the foot of Fore Street, car No 12 left the rails, swerved to the right and overturned. No lifting gear was available, so bit by bit it was dismantled in situ and carried away to the scrap yard.

By 1933 a comprehensive network of bus services was in operation throughout the City, the routes being designated by letters instead of service numbers, a practice which continues to the present day. At the outbreak of war in 1939, the City transport department possessed a modern fleet of vehicles, in smart green and cream livery, with no advertisements on the outside panels; they were a credit to any transport undertaking and in keeping with the general standard of City life at that period. During World War II all single deck buses were converted to ARP ambulances and were called into use in that capacity during the savage Baedeker air raids on Exeter during April and May 1942, when whole areas of the historic heart of the City were devasted by fire and high explosive bombs. Being situated away from the centre, neither the Corporation Transport depot nor the Devon General garage was damaged by these air raids, but for several days after, the City streets were in complete chaos, with constant diversions due to collapsed buildings and the discovery of unexploded bombs.

During 1946, as industry began to return to normal after wartime conditions, new buses were obtained and the switch from petrol to oil engined vehicles was completed.

Although the 1947 Joint Transport agreement covered a ten mile radius from Exeter, as far as fares were concerned, the policy of a separate scale (based on mileage) for the lettered city services continued until 1970 while the normal Devon General country scale applied in those areas outside the City but within the joint area. The type of vehicle operated in Exeter was the conventional vertical front engined, open rear platform, double decker but recent years have seen innovations with the introduction of twin exit/entrance single manned, under floor engined single deckers on certain city and country routes. In 1968 Devon General acquired a number of front entrance, large capacity, Leyland Atlantean double deckers for use on City routes.

During the late 1960s Exeter Corporation encountered difficulties in working the joint agreement and the transport undertaking incurred recurrent deficits. As a result the Corporation gave notice in 1969 of its intention to terminate the agreement by 31 March 1970 and to seek a new and more favourable scheme. In the interim, however, the Transport Act of 1968 came into effect enabling local authorities to dispose of their transport undertakings, if desired. As a result, Exeter City decided to sell its bus system to the National Bus Company with effect from 1 April 1970. Placed under Devon General control the former Exeter City buses retained their green and cream livery until mid 1971 when they began to be repainted in Devon General maroon livery. More recently with the transfer of Devon General to Western National the former Exeter City fleet bears the new poppy red NBC livery of Devon General and the legal ownership of Western National. The standard Devon General town service fare scale is now applicable in Exeter City.

Devon General from 1947

The immediate post war years saw a rapid expansion of bus traffic, due to restrictions on private motoring resulting from petrol rationing. On many Devon General routes, single deckers were replaced by larger capacity double deckers. By 1956 the recession of traffic was beginning to make itself felt and Devon General introduced its first one man operated buses on country routes. This trend has continued with new single deck one man buses replacing double deck crew operated buses. On the other hand, in town areas peak traffic periods in the morning and afternoons have tended to increase, with more scholars travelling to centralised schools and a fairly high level of employment generally. To meet this need and avoid the use of duplicate vehicles, Devon General has brought into operation large capacity double deckers in the Torbay and Exeter town areas many of which are one-man operated.

From 1950 onward Devon General developed its properties by building new bus stations at Paignton in 1954 (used jointly with Western National), followed by Brixham in 1957, while in 1960 the new bus station and adjacent garage at Newton Abbot allowed the closure of the old garage at Kingsteignton. Finally, in 1964, the fine new bus and coach station at Paris Street, Exeter, replaced the overcrowded site at Paul Street.

Pursuing its policy of buying out as many local operators as possible in order to give unrestricted scope to the economic planning of services and fare fixing, Devon General has purchased a number of businesses since 1948, as listed in Appendix C.

The business of H. D. Gourd & Son acquired in 1955 deserves special mention, as Harold D. Gourd commenced operation as early as 1896 with a horse wagon between Bishopsteignton and Teignmouth for both passengers and freight. The first motor bus, a Daimler 14 seater, was acquired in 1914, giving Gourds the distinction of being the pioneer motor bus operator in the area. This bus ceased operation while Mr Gourd was in France during World War I, but Mrs Gourd carried on with the horse bus. After the war, the Daimler resumed operation and the service was gradually built up, Mr Gourd's sons becoming drivers and supplying the '& Sons' portion of the firm's title. From the beginning, Mr Gourd had a parcel carrying contract with the GWR and later this required a special van, as the number of parcels could not be accommodated on the buses. From 1931 until the business was sold in 1955, all new vehicles were Bedford. The two stage services are now merged and operated by Devon General as Newton Abbot-Bishopsteignton-Teignmouth.

Another operation deserving special mention was Mr Potter's Tor Bus Service, which commenced in 1921 with an open Ford T lorry with improvised bench seats, working between Liverton and Newton Abbot. In 1925 a Dodge 14 seater was purchased and two years later the route was extended to Haytor and Widecombe-in-the-Moor and the name Tor Bus was adopted. During the 1940–50 period the service was maintained by Leyland Cubs and traffic was so plentiful in those days that duplicates crammed to the doors with passengers and goods, could be seen grinding up the steep hills to Haytor. However the growth of private car traffic, particularly for visitors to Dartmoor, brought about the withdrawal of Mr Potter's service in 1963. To meet local requests, Devon General agreed to fill the gap with a shopping bus, which started in June 1964 and still operates between Newton Abbot and Haytor on Wednesdays, Fridays and Saturdays only.

5 Greenslades Tours and National Travel

If the Greenslade Brothers' slogan for success had been 'Don't bother to train, be coached by us' it would have been perfectly understandable. For when school-leaver Gilbert Greenslade presented himself at Exeter St David's station to seek a job with the Great Western Railway, he was turned down flat.

It may have had something to do with the standard of his mental arithmetic at the time, but the fact remains that the railways turned their backs on this future Mayor of Exeter who, with his two brothers, William and Percy, was to build up a coach business which became the envy of their competititors in later years.

Their father, Mr Samuel James Greenslade came from Shobrooke, near Crediton, and was for many years a railway signalman at Hele and Bradninch station. Mr and Mrs Samuel Greenslade had five children—three sons and two daughters. The eldest, William, was born in 1894 and on leaving school joined Davey's Cycle Works in Cowick Street, Exeter, to train as a cycle mechanic. His youngest brother, Percy, received similar training later, which was to stand them in good stead in 1912 when the Bradninch family entered the business arena by hiring out bicycles at 3d an hour or 6d an hour with tuition!

Greenslade Brothers' first motor vehicle was a Model T Ford, acquired in 1912 and two years later they purchased a Mass French char-a-banc. But the war clouds were gathering and leaving their sister, Evelyn, to look after their business interests, the brothers answered the call to the colours.

William began by driving an ambulance in France and incidentally, Bill Lang—who was later to become Chief Engineer of Greenslades Tours Ltd—served with him. Later William joined the Flying Corps where he obtained his wings as a pilot. Gilbert served with the 4th Devon Regiment for two years and then he too joined the Flying Corps and was training to be a pilot when the war ended. The youngest brother, Percy, served as an aero-mechanic.

After the war the three brothers pooled their gratuities which they used as capital, ploughing their profits back into the business. Gilbert Greenslade has no hesitation in admitting that they were helped by the rail strike of 1921 and the general strike of 1926, when they drove day and night in their search for business.

The Greenslades left Bradninch in 1920, when they purchased a house and some stables—part of Collins Horse Repository—in Paris Street, Exeter. They expanded the premises by acquiring some gardens; during their excavation of the gardens a neighbouring house fell down! It is on this same site, immediately opposite the entrance to Exeter coach station, that the City's new civic centre has been built today. In the early 1920s Greenslades' office was part of the kitchen in their Paris Street house but in 1925 they acquired the lease of 10 Queen Street—previously used as a fish shop. This was, however, but a temporary measure, for the City Council which owned the premises were anxious to redevelop Exeter's 'Golden Heart', which was not in fact carried out until 1976!

They next moved to 84 Queen Street where they remained until May 1942 when the City was bombed. During the blitz, Exeter's general post office was destroyed and numbers 84 and 85 Queen Street were commandeered for a temporary postal headquarters.

At this stage, 14 Queen Street became the registered office of Greenslades Tours Ltd and remained until 1964 when the

Company moved to headquarters at 29 Paris Street. Meanwhile, the engineering department had left Paris Street in 1961 to take up residence in the new garage and workshops at Willey's Avenue.

The expansion of the Greenslade Brothers' business began in 1932 when they took over Empress Coaches of Teignmouth, Milton Services of Crediton and The Witheridge Transport Co Ltd (disposed of to Devon General in 1948 see Appendix C). Between 1936 and 1947 the following businesses were acquired: Regent Coaches (Teignmouth) Ltd; Arcadia Coach Tours and Miller's Tours, both of Exmouth. In October 1953 Greenslades became a BET subsidiary and the expansion of the business continued with the takeover of the following: Taylor's Central Garage of Exeter; Teign Cars of Teignmouth; Burgoyne's Tours of Sidmouth; Knight's Tours of Exeter; Dagworthy's Coaches of Sidmouth; Blue Moorland Coaches of Dawlish and Hart's Tours of Budleigh Salterton. When the Company became part of the BET organisation, Mr Percy Greenslade went into retirement but his two brothers joined the Greenslades Board of Directors.

Mr William Greenslade served in this capacity for three years before giving up his seat on the Board. In 1963 he went back into business on his own account when he acquired Clatworthy's Tours of Tiverton. He actively directed operations under the name of 'W. J. Greenslade's Tours' until his death in June 1968.

Alderman Gilbert Greenslade retained his seat on the Board from 1953 until December 1973, during which period the Company passed from the ownership of BET to the Transport Holding Company and then became part of the National Bus Company when it was set up on 1 January 1969. Gilbert Greenslade has been active in public life since 1937 when he was first elected to serve on the Exeter City Council. He was appointed Sheriff of Exeter for the year

149

1950–51 and became Mayor of the City in 1955–56.

As a result of the NBC ownership of the former BET companies, there was a considerable degree of integration between Western/Southern National, Devon General and Greenslades. During the 1969 season the day and half day excursions programmes of Greenslades and Grey Cars from Exeter and Exmouth were amalgamated to provide more economical utilisation of coaches and staff. The success of this pilot scheme resulted in the Grey Cars business of Devon General being transferred to Greenslades Tours Ltd on 2 May 1971. Under this scheme Greenslades would probably have become an area office of Western National but all this was to change with the establishment in April 1972 of the Central Activities Group (CAG) of the National Bus Company. One of its main objectives was the integration and development of coach operation for marketing on a national scale, which hitherto had been operated either by individual subsidiary companies or by groups working together under joint arrangements. Broadly this involved the establishment of a national network of express coach services and the bringing together of various extended tour programmes as 'National Holidays'. Initially the organisation was based on five area companies, but in 1977 they were reduced to four, although the company relevant to this history, National Travel (South West) Ltd, was not affected by this reorganisation. An important step was the adoption of a common national white livery for coaches engaged on the main express services and inclusive tours.

One of the significant aspects of the new organisation was that a number of NBC subsidiary coach companies were transferred to CAG control. The secretary of Black & White Motorways became secretary of Greenslades, and over a period of months the two companies became more closely related until both became part of National Travel (South West) Ltd on 1 January 1974. The final change took place on

14 July 1974 when Greenslades engineering control passed from Western National to the National Travel (South West) Ltd chief engineer at Cheltenham.

As a result of an application to the Traffic Commissioners in 1973, Greenslades was authorised to pick up passengers in Plymouth on its extended holiday tours and in April 1974 based two coaches at the BRS (Parcels) Ltd depot at Plympton, near Plymouth. Further vehicles were allocated in order to assist Western National in the operation of its local tours from Plymouth. Coaches were also provided for the National Express network and soon enquiries began to come in from prospective private hire clients. Subsequently the coaches were housed at the NCL depot in Plymouth.

In 1977 Greenslades transferred its Sidmouth tours licence to Western National and subsequently the depot and enquiry office were sold. The more important change came on 16 April 1978 when the Greenslades offices at Teignmouth, Dawlish Warren, Babbacombe and in Torquay (except Vaughan Parade office which was retained by Greenslades) were transferred to Western National, together with fifteen coaches (8 Bedford YRT 360-367, 6 Bristol LHS 317-322, and 1 Bedford VAS 351). The Greenslades depots at Dawlish, Exmouth and Teignmouth had been closed in 1975. To complete the reorganisation Western National applied to the Traffic Commissioners for the relative Greenslades road service licences in Torbay and in effect the former Grey Cars business, with the addition of Teignmouth and Dawlish, returned to Devon General under which name the coach business trades in Torbay. At the same time Greenslades ceased trading in Plymouth.

For a number of reasons Greenslades Tours retains its trading name although its assets are wholly owned by National Travel (South West) Ltd. At the time of writing the company has a fleet of 36 coaches with main depot and office at Exeter, and booking offices at Exmouth and Torquay. Over the past 20 years Greenslades specialised in the field of inclusive holiday tours with picking-up points throughout the South West, conveying an average 20,000 passengers per year. Continental tours were developed until 1969 when, by arrangement with Wallace Arnold Tours (Devon) Ltd, Greenslades transferred its continental tour licences to Wallace Arnold. As a result of applications to the Traffic Commissioners Greenslades regained its continental licences in 1974 and since that date has maintained a comprehensive programme of tours of short duration to the continent. Details of Wallace Arnold's coaching activities in the South West are given in Chapter 6.

From an operational standpoint, the Greenslades business continues to provide a wide and varied programme of day tours and excursions in addition to its private hire activities. Coaches are still operated on extended holiday tours but the brand name is now National Holidays, and Greenslades is an operating participant, along with many of the other NBC subsidiary companies.

The supervision of overall planning of the holidays is carried out on a centralised basis but within each National Travel area there are specialist staff who assist in the planning for the area's own known market and then combine with the other areas in producing a finished programme. At the inception of the National Holiday scheme the Greenslades organisation was expanded as the tours planning section of National Travel (South West) Ltd, covering South Wales and the West Country. The staff at Exeter were responsible for the planning of holiday tours operated by Greenslades Tours, Hants & Dorset Motors Service Ltd of Bournemouth, Wessex National of Bristol (former Wessex Coaches Ltd), Shamrock & Rambler Motor Coaches of Bournemouth, Western Welsh Omnibus Co Ltd of Cardiff, and the South Wales Transport Co Ltd of Swansea. This arrangement continued until October 1977 when a new National Holidays

Division centralised at Sheffield became responsible for co-ordinating the planning, adminstration, and marketing of National Holidays on a national basis.

A tours unit is maintained in Swansea to supervise the charting of tours originating in South Wales and a similar function for the other companies is carried out at Exeter where the tours staff are housed at National House, Queen Street, Exeter, having formerly been located at offices in Musgrave House, Musgrave Row, Exeter.

National Travel is also responsible for operating the national network of express coach services, formerly operated by individual bus and coach companies. Among these were Royal Blue, Bristol Onmibus Company, Red & White, Black & White and of course Associated Motorways. Now planning, marketing and charting are the responsibility of National Travel, with the individual companies providing coaches and drivers. In the South West the principle centre of control is Cheltenham, where planning and allied functions are carried out, together with charting and the actual operation of a large number of the services. Exeter is the other important centre in relation to charting and operation, the chart room for the West Country being located in the Coach Station at Paris Street.

The establishment of the Exeter express coach control centre has resulted in the chart rooms at Bournemouth and Taunton being closed and the charting functions previously carried out at London (Victoria Coach Station) being transferred to Exeter or Cheltenham. With the responsibility for the planning of services undertaken by National Travel, which is now the licence holder, the opportunity has been taken to develop the express service network for the conditions of the 1970s and to make use of the developing motorway network in the South West.

Further integration has taken place in recent years and all former Royal Blue inspectors at Exeter, Bournemouth,

Salisbury, Southampton, and London are now on the staff of National Travel. Bournemouth Square bus and coach station was the scene of a disastrous fire in 1976 which resulted in National Express services operating from the Shamrock & Rambler garage at 79 Holdenhurst Road, Bournemouth, a move which started a train of events which resulted in all traffic staff of Royal Blue at Bournemouth together with drivers transferring to National Travel from May 1977. As the Portsmouth operation of Royal Blue had been transferred to National Travel in May 1976 the only remaining components of the extensive Royal Blue organisation are drivers at Exeter, and a few clerical staff and drivers at London. Moreover Western National and Devon General staff from many of their home depots operate an extensive portion of the National Express mileage in the South West. National Travel also has its own express units at Swansea, Tredegar, Bristol, Exeter (based on Greenslades) and Cheltenham so that the policy of rationalisation and transfer in the South West is nearly complete.

What have these changes achieved from the point of view of the user? In the first place the common identity of coaches in the smart white livery has enabled a common marketing approach to be adopted, with a corporate identity used in signing, publicity, uniforms and buildings. Dramatic changes have taken place in the services operated which in the West Country are related to four daily regular long distance routes to London, with extensive interchange facilities at key points. The main service came into operation on 28 September 1975 and is named the *Western Venturer*. It links London with Bristol every 90 minutes, with alternate journeys proceeding to either Weston-super-Mare or to Taunton, Exeter and Plymouth. Connecting coaches developed from the traditional Royal Blue idea provide a comprehensive network of services throughout the West Country.

On 26 September 1976 two more named services were

154

introduced, the *Cotswold Sovereign* from Gloucester to London via Cheltenham and the *Southern Mariner* from Bournemouth, via Southampton to London. Whilst not strictly relevant to this history, but for the sake of completeness the fourth named service is *Y Ddraig Goch, The Red Dragon*, from South Wales to London. All these services make extensive use of motorways with fast timings—eg Exeter to Cheltenham is covered in 2½ hours. While coaches from the different units retain their traditional fleet names (Black & White, Greenslades, Shamrock & Rambler and Wessex National) for their domestic activities in order to retain the personal touch and goodwill attached to these companies, the fleet name 'South West' is used on the area's express coaches as part of the marketing image for the area as a whole. The combined area fleet is 205 coaches and in recent years new vehicles have been Leyland Leopards and Bedfords, although there have been a small number of new AEC but they were not allocated to Greenslades which, for many years, was a major operator of AEC vehicles.

Hiring of outside operators at peak periods is now the function of National Travel and the principle offices are connected by Telex. While all these changes have meant a reduction in the number of administrative staff required, the scope of the National Bus Company has meant that redundant staff have in general either been absorbed by natural wastage, or appointed to vacant posts in other departments or companies.

A restructuring of NBC regions (stage carriage services) took place in September 1977 and at the same time the Regional Directors in England assumed the chairmanship of the National Travel area companies in their Regions. The two main objectives of the reorganisation are to achieve full co-operation between Regional and National Travel companies and to ensure the most efficient and economical use of vehicles in all coach operations throughout the Group.

6 Independent Operators

Despite the extensive acquisitions made by the major bus companies in the 1920s and 1930s, there are still a number of independent operators of local bus services throughout the South West. They are either people who despite the competition or tempting offers of the large bus groups preferred to continue running their own small businesses, or operators who found niches between the territorial boundaries of the major companies, or sparsely populated districts which did not interest the larger companies.

In the territory of Devon General there are only one or two independents left, but Western National, with its sprawling sparsely populated territory still has some 90 small stage operators scattered throughout its system. A complete list of acquired independent operators within the area covered by this book will be found in Appendix B, but it is the intention of this chapter to select certain areas, which are still predominantly served by private operators and say something about the fortunes of the small bus businesses which have served them over the past 100 years.

South East Somerset and North Dorset

South of the Bristol Omnibus Company's territory at Warminster-Frome-Shepton Mallet and extending southward to Dorchester—an area some 15 miles from east to west and 30 miles from north to south—lies an enclave served by local operators, apart from Western National routes radiating from Yeovil depot.

One of the principal stage carriage businesses is that of Hutchings & Cornelius Services Ltd of South Petherton.

This was formed in 1934 from an amalgamation of two previous operators who had started up some 10 years earlier, Cornelius Services of Barrington, with services from Barrington to Taunton and Ilminster to Yeovil (via Barrington, Kingsbury Episcopi and Tintinhull), and Hutchings Omnibus Service of South Petherton (the registered offices of the present company) with services from South Petherton to Yeovil and Chiselborough to Yeovil. When registered in 1934 the company had nine buses (eight Thorneycroft and one Dennis), four of which were garaged at Barrington and five at South Petherton. The original livery was cream and black but this rather sombre colouring was changed in 1943 to light blue with grey lining. By 1954 the original founders, Thomas Hutchings and Alfred Cornelius, had both died and the Vincent family of Yeovil (who had been represented on the board of directors since 1934) took over. The present directors are S. H. Vincent (Chairman), S. H. Vincent and P. H. Vincent. The new owners changed the livery once again, to red and cream. By 1964 the fleet totalled 21 vehicles, mainly Dennis Lancets, the policy being to purchase new vehicles for coach work and transfer them to stage operation after three years. In 1965 the policy was changed and it was decided to standardise on AEC chassis and to keep the coach fleet separate from the bus fleet. The livery was again altered, this time to maroon and cream for buses and carnation red and ermine white for coaches. In common with all operators with a preponderance of stage service commitments, the decline in passengers necessitated a general overhaul of operations in 1970, as a result of which the Barrington-Taunton service was withdrawn (subsequently reinstated on Saturdays between Westport and Taunton), the Ilminster-Tintinhull-Yeovil service reduced to Fridays only and the express service to Westland Works, Yeovil cancelled, together with two school contracts in the Yeovil area. These reductions enabled Barrington depot to be closed and the fleet to be reduced to 16 vehicles. All buses are one man operated; school contracts, private hire and excursions and tours are also carried out.

During 1978, as a result of an overall settlement between Hutchings & Cornelius and Western National, the latter withdrew its service 466 Yeovil-South Petherton, leaving Hutchings & Cornelius to exploit the full potentials of the route. For some years it had become apparent that there was insufficient traffic potential to justify two major operators. Services currently in operation are South Petherton-Yeovil— 12 journeys weekdays; Crewkerne-Chiselborough-Yeovil—4 journeys weekdays; South Petherton-Langport-Taunton— 4 journeys weekdays; Ilminster-Barrington-Kingsbury Episcopi-Tintinhull-Yeovil—Fridays only; Westport-Isle Abbots-Taunton—Saturdays only, 1 journey.

As this book goes to press comes the unexpected news that Hutchings & Cornelius ceased trading on 31 May 1979, being unable to keep pace with increasing costs. The services will be continued by other operators.

Further south at Cattistock in Dorset is situated the older business of A. Pearce & Co Ltd. A few days after the 1918 Armistice, Albert Pearce purchased a local coal round and with a mule and cart and a van set up as village carrier. He went into Dorchester on market days (Wednesdays and Saturdays) going round villages to take shopping orders and stopping at any house displaying a large 'P'; the first day's takings were 3s 6d (17½p). As business was brisk, a serving soldier (George Collins) and his horse were hired in 1919 and George Collins returned to the business after leaving the services and married Mr Pearce's daughter in 1923. Meanwhile in the early 1920s an ex-army Albion and a Ford 30 cwt truck were purchased being supplemented in 1923 by another Ford truck and a 14 seat Ford bus. The bus made its twice weekly journey into Dorchester, often with more parcels than passengers and for the rest of the week its seats were

(*above*) Leyland National No 2845 is representative of a large number of similar buses which entered service with both the green (Western National) and red (Devon General) fleets during the late 1970s (*Western National*); (*below*) rear view of one of Trathens Plaxton-bodied Volvos, photographed in 1976 near the eastern frontier of Turkey with Mount Ararat in the background. (*Collection of Trathens Coaches*)

((top left) Mr Alfred Pearce and his 1923 Ford bus at Cattistock, 1948. (*A Pearce*); (*top right*) Bedford operated by Tally Ho! on a former Western National stage service from Kingsbridge. (*R C Anderson*); (*above*) Bere Regis & District Motor Service AEC Reliance coach with 51 seat Duple Viceroy body. (*Bere Regis*); (*below*) one of Pearce's Bedford/Duple buses at Trinity Street Yard, Dorchester, 1955, with an older vehicle in the background. These are typical of the vehicles once used by independent coach operators in rural areas (*A Pearce*)

removed and it was used to deliver coal or move furtniture!

By 1925 business was prospering and Albert Pearce formed a partnership with his daughter (Mrs E. Collins) and son in law. A new site was purchased and the present garage constructed in 1926. In 1929 a new Ford 14 seater with upholstered seats was acquired and the Dorchester service was increased to twice on Wednesdays and three journeys on Saturdays. During the 1930s the firm concentrated mainly on haulage and it was not until 1937 that its last horse drawn van ceased to operate. A school contract was obtained in 1932 and another in 1934 necessitating the purchase of a second bus—a 1929 20 seat Reo with gold crown engine (the band bus of the Irish Guards!). Tours were also commenced to three destinations (Weymouth, Bournemouth and Tidworth Tattoo). The buses continued to operate throughout the 1939–45 War, although the Reo was replaced in 1944 by a 20 seat Dennis Ace. Albert Pearce 'retired' in 1942 aged 65 but continued to help owing to wartime staff shortages, and in fact drove for another ten years. In 1947 a pre war Bedford was purchased for the growing tours business which then comprised 12 destinations, increased the following year to 32. George Collins unfortunately died in 1948 and his son Ivor, the present director, took over the business.

Meanwhile in the 1920s Frank Legg had begun operating a bus from Evershot to Dorchester on Wednesdays and Saturdays, to Yeovil on Mondays, Wednesdays and Fridays and later to Sherborne on Thursdays. Although running over the same route as Pearce there was no friction between the two operators, both of whom thrived. At Sydling, nearby, Frank Tyrell also had a bus, which was sold in rapid succession to Mr Kelloway and then to Jimmy Crabb, who also delivered coal in his bus. Tyrell promptly set up in business again and for years Sydling had the luxury of two public carriers. Residents of Grimstone and Stratton, where all the operators converged, had five different services into Dor-

chester (the fifth being Cox of Frampton); the only drawback
was that they all ran in a bunch at much about the same time!
A sixth carrier, Jack Record of Rampisham stuck to his horse
and van until well into the 1940s. All were members of the
Dorchester & District Carriers' Association who printed their
tickets and a common timetable for the Dorchester area.

After the war, matters began to sort themselves out; Tyrell
sold to Albert Lovell who in turn bought out Crabb and then
sold out to Pearce in 1951. Meanwhile Cox sold to Frank
Whitty, who in turn was acquired by Bere Regis & District
Motor Services. Legg continued until 1954 when he decided
to concentrate on haulage and Pearce took over his bus
services. The various services between Yeovil, Cattistock and
Dorchester were co-ordinated and reconstituted under one
new through licence, Yeovil-Dorchester; the three tour
licences were also combined with unspecified picking-up
points within a six-mile radius and many more destinations
were added.

During the early 1950s when bus traffic was at its peak,
several other local stage services were started but all were later
abandoned owing to declining traffic. Albert Pearce died in
1955. In the same year, daily (except Sundays) morning and
evening buses were started for workers between Cattistock
and Dorchester, which have continued to thrive to the
present day. Foreseeing the decline in stage carriage traffic,
Pearce's concentrated on school contracts and in 1957 built
additional workshops for repairs to private cars (to offset loss
of passengers on the buses). The business was incorporated as
a limited company in 1963 with Mrs E. Collins, Mrs H.
Collins and Ivor J. Collins as directors. Three years later
railway stations and halts between Yeovil and Dorchester
were closed and to meet the needs of intermediate villages
the bus service into Dorchester was augmented. Finally,
in 1970 several extended tours were added to the licence.
From two buses in 1949, Mr Collins and his ladies have

developed their business and fleet to the present 13 vehicles. The firm has built up a fine record with its employees and there is very little turnover of staff, some of whom have been with Pearce & Co for over 25 years.

Three other operators in this area have been in the bus business for some 40 years—

Wakes Services (Sparkford) Ltd., 25 vehicles (21 coaches and 4 buses of AEC and Bedford) on contracts, tours and the following bus services:

Sparkford-Lovington-Wraxall-Evercreech-Shepton Mallet.
  1 journey Fridays only
Yeovil-Sparkford-Babcary-Keinton-Mandeville.
  1 journey Wednesdays and Saturdays
Yeovil-Sparkford-Castle Cary-Evercreech-Shepton Mallet.
  5 journeys weekdays
Castle Cary-Sparkford-Sherborne.
  4 journeys on Pack Monday Fair Day at Sherborne only

Wakes, in common with all other stage operators, has had to contend with declining traffic and six market services have been abandoned.

H. R. & V. Gunn, South Petherton, 10 vehicles (2 Bedford, 3 AEC, 4 Leyland, 1 Volvo) on tours, contracts and one regular stage service South Petherton-Crewkerne-Yeovil (weekdays, 7 journeys). Commenced in 1928.

N. A., H. M. & M. D. House, Hilton, Blandford, 5 Bedford vehicles on contracts and two regular stage services: Milton Abbas-Hilton-Puddletown-Dorchester (weekdays) and Hilton-Blandford (Thursdays only).

No account of bus transport in this area would be complete without mention of Bere Regis & District Motor Services of Dorchester, a partnership of three local operators (Messrs Toop, Ironside and Davis) formed in 1936. Mr R. W. Toop started to operate weekly market buses between Bere

Regis and Poole, Wareham, Wimborne and Dorchester in
1929. He was joined in 1930 by Mr W. J. Ironside with
services from Winfrith to Dorchester, Wareham and Weymouth and finally in 1936 by Mr P. W. Davis, who for ten
years had been operating between Poole and Dorchester.
The three partners rapidly absorbed most of the other small
carriers and bus businesses in north east Dorset and the
undertaking now has 86 vehicles. The greater part are
engaged on private hire and contract work but the undertaking has some 17 stage services radiating from Dorchester,
Sturminster Newton, Bere Regis and Blandford. The previous
double deck route from Bere Regis to Poole and Dorchester
was taken over by Hants & Dorset and Southern National
All three of the original partners have now died.

Other operators within the area under review are:

S. S. & B. E. Smith of Batcombe, 11 vehicles on tours,
contacts and the following bus services:
Bruton-Upton Noble-Frome: 1 journey Wednesdays only
Batcombe-Alham-Shepton Mallet: 1 journey, Fridays only
Frome-Bruton-Cole (School days)
Fourfoot Cross-Parbrook-Pylle-Pilton-Shepton Mallet: 1
journey Fridays.
Frome-Wanstrow-Upton-Noble-Batcombe-Alham-Doult-
ing-Shepton Mallet: weekdays

E. W. Gould of Pilton, nine vehicles on tours from Shepton
Mallet and Pilton, and contracts.

The business of A. E. Faulkner of Marnhull, a relative
newcomer (1969) who was operating services between
Sturminster Newton-Shaftesbury and Sturminster Newton-
Gillingham was replaced in 1977 by Shaftesbury & District
Motor Services (R. S. Brown & Light) which now operates
an extensive network of rural routes in the Shaftesbury area.

Central Devon

The area bounded by Crediton, Tiverton, Dulverton, South Molton, Torrington, Holsworthy, Launceston and Oke-hampton, some 35 miles from west to east and 20 miles from north to south, is one of diminutive market towns and remote scattered villages, where the population shows a general decline at each census. Apart from Western National's Bideford-Exeter service which cuts right across this area, and the small Devon General outstation at Witheridge, with services to Tiverton, Crediton and Exeter, the bus services of the region always have been run by small operators.

South Molton, in the north of this area, is the headquarters of Terraneau's Garage, established in 1903 as cycle and car dealers. John Terraneau, the present general manager, is the third generation of that name to be engaged in the garage and bus business, his mother Mrs H. Terraneau (widow of W. H. M. Terraneau who died in 1968) being the proprietor of the firm. The coach fleet consists of 10 vehicles. Six stage carriage services are operated:

South Molton—East Anstey. Tuesdays & Thursdays.
    (Rail replacement service).
South Molton—Barnstaple via Chittlehampton.
    1 journey Fridays.
South Molton—Roachill. Thursdays.
South Molton—George Nympton. Thursdays and school
    days.
South Molton—Brayford—Barnstaple.
    Thursdays and Fridays.
Chittlehampton—South Molton—Exeter.
    Every 4th Saturday.
South Molton—Filleigh. Thursdays and school days.
North Molton—Nadrid Cross. School days.
North Molton—Brayford—Exeter. Saturdays.
Barnstaple—West Buckland. Fridays.

165

Terraneau also operates six school contracts and one private contract and holds a tours licence from South Molton.

A little further south, at Chulmleigh, is the business of A. Turner, who has driven his own buses for over 50 years. Mr Turner was one of those pioneers who fought in World War I and afterwards spent his gratuity on the purchase of a Thorneycroft lorry with solid tyres, which he transformed into a bus and started his first journey from Chulmleigh to Exeter in July 1920. At first weekly, the service now runs on three days per week.

The original Thorneycroft was replaced by a Dennis, a service to Barnstaple was also started up and by 1930 six vehicles were employed on both regular bus services and private hire work. At this time Mr Turner obtained a Foden steam engine wagon and started heavy goods haulage to supplement the passenger side of his business which continues, consisting mainly in the transport of wood from the mid-Devon forestry plantations to pulp mills. Mrs Turner has been a loyal supporter throughout her life and still accompanies her husband on the market buses. The present fleet consists of 13 vehicles including a 1977 registered Bedford YMT3/Duple 53 seater. Besides excursions and tours from Chulmleigh, the following stage services are operated:

Kings Nympton-Chulmleigh-Lapford-Exeter: (Tuesdays, Fridays and Saturdays)
Chulmleigh-Kings Nympton-South Molton: (Thursdays)
Lapford-Chulmleigh-Umberleigh-Barnstaple: (Fridays)
Chulmleigh-Dolton-Beaford-Yarnscombe-Barnstaple: (Fridays)

In the north west corner of the area, with headquarters at the tiny hamlet of Stibb Cross, is the business of E. W. Jones, taken over from J. K. Slade, who in turn took over in 1969 from Mrs Hill, widow of Samuel Hill who died in 1968. Sam

Hill, like Mr Turner, was one of the old pioneers of bus transport, who started up 50 years ago and was originally a body builder as well as bus operator. The firm now owns 15 vehicles and besides excursions and tours with picking up points at seven neighbouring villages, and school contracts, has eight stage services, all of the market type:

Stibb Cross-Bideford via Main Road: Tuesdays and Saturdays

Stibb Cross-Shebbear-Holsworthy: Wednesdays only

Stibb Cross-Shebbear-Black Torrington-Hatherleigh-Bow-Crediton-Exeter: Mondays and Fridays.

Stibb Cross-Bulkworthy-Putford-Bideford: Saturdays

Stibb Cross-Shebbear-Torrington-Bideford: Saturdays only

Stibb Cross-Shebbear-Stibb Cross-Bideford: Tuesdays only

Stibb Cross-Frithelstock-Torrington: Saturdays only.

Completing the pattern of transport in the northern half of this area was the long established business of Mr Wills of Atherington which was taken over in 1976 by Mr R. J. Buse. The five vehicles. were largely occupied on contracts, private hires and tours, and the only stage carriage commitment was a market service on Tuesdays and Fridays from Burrington via High Bickington, Atherington and Chapelton to Barnstaple.

Turning to the south of this area of Devon, there are only two long established operators, whose businesses can be traced back to the days between the two World Wars. First, Mr E. Saunders of Winkleigh, whose five Bedford vehicles (some of them vintage models) are engaged on school contracts and on two market services between Winkleigh and Exeter, on Thursdays via Wembworthy and Morchard Road, and Fridays via Coldridge and Morchard Road. Second is Mr Hookway of Meeth who has six vehicles largely employed on contracts and private hire, but with one stage service from Meeth via Morton, Petrockstow, Marland, Winswell and Torrington to Bideford on Tuesdays and Saturdays only, and a local journey on Thursdays between Taddiport and Torrington, and a summer Sunday service to Westward Ho!

Mr N. C. Born of Northlew, until recently ran all the public transport facilities from that large village. In January 1971 the business was transferred to W. J. Jordan and in 1977 to F. R. Guscott; 11 vehicles are involved and four stage services are in operation:

Northlew-Waytown-Okehampton (Wednesday and
    Saturdays)
Northlew-Hatherleigh-Highampton-Sheepwash-Black
    Torrington-Halwill-Beaworthy-Bratton Clovelly-
    Lewdon-Lewtrenchard-Tavistock-Plymouth (Thurdays
    and second Saturday in month)
Northlew-Exeter (Last Friday in each alternate month).
    Licensed as an express service.
Okehampton-Northlew-Sheepwash-Black Torrington
    (First Saturday in month).

Mr Elven (Okeridge Motor Services) of Okehampton, has appeared on the scene since World War II, principally through the acquisition of a former operator on the trunk route, Okehampton-Hatherleigh-Meeth-Merton-Torrington-Bideford. The former Southern National also sold its interests on this road to Mr Elven in 1966. Okeridge Motor Services also runs journeys on Tuesdays, Thursdays and Saturdays between Okehampton-Sampford Courtenay and North Tawton, and on school days on a circular route from Oke-hapton via Belstone and Sticklepath. There are also summer only services (when the weather is fine and the military are not firing guns!) into the heart of Dartmoor (Okement Hill), and recently, an Okehampton-Tavistock-Plymouth service

168

has been introduced on Tuesdays and a Torrington-Barnstaple service on Fridays. This little network of services, together with works contracts, occupies a fleet of four vehicles.

At Halwill, F. R. Guscott referred to above also operates four vehicles in an area of sparse declining population on the following four stage services:

Halwill-Quoditch-Ashwater-Tetcott-Clawton-
  Holsworthy: Wednesdays
Halwill-Hunscott-Ashwater-Broadwoodwidger-Lifton
  Down-Launceston: Tuesdays only.
Halwill-Ashwater-Broadwoodwidger-Lifton-Lewdown-
  Tavistock-Plymouth: Second Friday in month.
Halwill-Okehampton: Second and Fourth Saturday in
  each month.

Finally, the thriving business of W. T. & W. R. & S. K. Phillips of North Tawton, completes the transport pattern of the area. Mr Phillips acquired the business of Mr G. E. Wright (Bow Belle) in 1966 who had himself taken over the long established firm of Mr. P W. Steer (Bow Belle) in 1958. The fleet has been expanded to 17 vehicles but the old fleet name of Bow Belle is still retained. The trunk service is from Okehampton via Sampford Courtenay, North Tawton, Bow, Copplestone and Crediton to Exeter, with deviations via Zeal Monachorum and Coleford on certain days. Excursions and tours are operated from North Tawton and Crediton.

Cornwall

In Cornwall there are over 30 operators of local stage services but they are scattered throughout the county and do not occupy any specific areas such as those already dealt with in this chapter. They range from one bus businesses, to Grenville Motor Services Ltd of Camborne which has 26 vehicles (including two double deckers). The latter company was formed just after World War II from an amalgamation of several long established operators, the business of T. W. Mundy (Silver Queen) of Camborne being added in 1965. In the last two or three years the small operators running buses on the Falmouth-Penryn town service have also been acquired by Grenville Motors. A number of important services are provided:

> Falmouth-Camborne: weekdays
> Falmouth-Penryn: daily
> Camborne-Troon: weekdays
> Redruth-Troon: Fridays
> Camborne-Leedstown-Penzance: weekdays
> Redruth-Nine Maidens: Fridays only
> Camborne-Pengegon circular: weekdays
> Four Lanes-Prah Sands: Tuesdays in August only
> Redruth-Portreath: weekdays
> Camborne-Helston: weekdays (ex Western National)

Wallace Arnold and Trathens

No chapter on independent operators of the South West would be complete without mention of the interests in Devon of Wallace Arnold Tours. It was 1947 when the Barr & Wallace Arnold Trust Limited acquired its first interest in the coach business in Torbay with the purchase of Waverley Motor Coach Tours Ltd, a small company operating four coaches on excursions and tours from Paignton. It was soon obvious to Robert Barr that there was a great future in this playground of the South West and in 1949 the shareholding of Ruby Tours Ltd (10 vehicles), one of the oldest coach operators in the West Country, was acquired. Waverley Coaches had been sub-contracting extensively to Ruby Tours throughout 1948 and it was obvious that it needed more licences and a better depot; with the acquisition of Ruby, Robert Barr got both. The business expanded when

Ruby Tours moved back into the Strand area early in the 1950s and in 1953 The Devon Touring Company ceased trading and sold its road service licences and one remaining vehicle to Wallace Arnold. Only two operators now remained in Paignton, Grey Cars the subsidiary of Devon General, and Wallace Arnold. Clearly Devon General had to take action to protect this very lucrative side of its business, for it commanded 60 per cent of all coach business in Torquay and Paignton, with 40 of the most modern AEC Duple coaches. In 1955 Devon General acquired A. E. Townsend of Babbacombe (10 coaches) and in 1956 Falkland Coaches (7 coaches). Wallace Arnold for its part was expanding, and in 1955 bought out Excelsior Motor Coach Tours (Torquay) Ltd (1 vehicle) owned by Mr R. J. Coombe.

In an effort to protect itself Cream Cars (Torquay) Ltd purchased Sunbeam Garages (Torquay) Ltd but unfortunately, the proprietor died very suddenly in 1957 and the business was purchased by Wallace Arnold, which by then had ceased trading as Ruby—Waverley—Devon Touring & Excelsior and had become one composite company, Wallace Arnold Tours (Devon) Ltd.

In 1966 with the last of the small operators in Torbay, Court Garages (Torquay) Ltd, sold to Devon General only two large operators were left, BET (Grey Cars) and the Barr & Wallace Arnold Trust with its subsidiary, Wallace Arnold Tours (Devon) Ltd, owning 30 modern luxury coaches, today the surviving independent operator.

As has been mentioned in Chapter 5, BET had been making progress in other areas and in 1953 purchased Greenslades Tours of Exeter. After the sale of BETs' bus and coach interests to the National Bus Company, Grey Cars with its long history was integrated with Greenslades Tours and the fleet livery changed first to the white and green of Greenslades and subsequently to the white of National Travel.

Wallace Arnold and Devon General both still strongly compete for excursion and tour traffic in the Torbay area and provide an excellent service to the public with day and half day trips all round the South West peninsula.

In 1974 Mr T. S. Congdon of the Embankment Motor Co (Plymouth) Ltd (27 coaches) died and the executors sold the Company to Wallace Arnold which was thus able to extend its tour operation in Devon to a second large base.

Yelverton near Plymouth is the base of one of the country's best known operators of Volvo coaches—F. G. Trathen & Son. Starting business in 1947 with one 'engineless' 20 seat coach purchased for £100 from the Embankment Motor Co, Plymouth, the firm next acquired three 25 seat coaches (in 1948/49/50) from Greenslades Tours Ltd, Exeter, and its first new 29 seat coach in 1950. In 1959 Trathen's expanded into continental private hire work and in 1968 obtained its first continental tours licence. Throughout the years Trathens has used various chassis and bodies, purchasing its first Volvo in 1974. Now the entire fleet is Volvo and by 1978 totalled some 30 coaches, all with Duple or Plaxton bodies. One coach has full air conditioning, toilet facilities, kitchenette area, stereo etc, and two executive coaches are similarly equipped but are not fully air-conditioned.

Today Trathens coaches go to Russia, Lapland, Austria, Italy, India, Pakistan, Afghanistan, and as far as Kashmir, besides the more usual Western European countries. At the other extreme Trathens operates local school contracts— with the same coaches! Such is the life of a coach operator— one day an extensive tour to the Indian sub-continent and on return—'the schools'!

172

7 Conclusions

The old pioneers who started up bus services did so as a means of making money. Life was simple and clear-cut; a bus was purchased, put on the road and if through competition or lack of passengers it did not pay, the service was promptly withdrawn. The question of social responsibility did not enter into the calculation, or if it did with some of the larger companies, it was secondary to, or a goodwill feature towards, producing a profit for the owner. This outlook remained the primary objective of bus operation until recent years. It is only in the past few years that a social pattern of increasing complexity, coupled with an increasing standard of living and a population which is rapidly becoming too large for the area in which it lives, has rendered the old clear-cut concepts of competition and profit a little out-of-date; it would be a mistake to say that they are no longer applicable but in future, particularly in the realms of transport, they must be coupled with other considerations.

The Road Traffic Act of 1930 has stood the test of nearly 50 years and throughout the preceding chapters its effect on the development and shape of the bus industry will have been apparent. The original intentions were confirmed in 1953 by a Royal Commission which investigated its workings. The Act provided that the Traffic Commissioners, in reaching their decisions, should have regard to the public interest and the needs of the area as a whole. This is the pivot on which the act works and which has contributed to its undoubted success. Although the Transport Act of 1978 has somewhat modified the powers of the Traffic Commissioners, it is difficult to contemplate a better objective.

The Transport Act 1968 enabled the Ministry of Transport to make grants towards the capital cost of new buses, provided they conformed to certain standard specifications, which placed emphasis on vehicles (both single and double-deck) for one-man operation. One-man operation is no new thing, dating back to the earliest days of bus transport as will be seen from reference in previous chapters of this book, but the wide-scale introduction of single manning on intensive city services, using double-deckers with sophisticated electronic ticket-issuing machines, is a new development; it is this aspect of general economy that the provisions of the Act are designed to promote. An important aspect of one-man operation is the easement of staff shortages; it also gives greater job satisfaction to the employee, which has many beneficial results not the least being a reduction in staff turnover. Labour costs represent more than 70 per cent of the operators' outgoings and anything which can help to keep this figure down, by increasing the productivity of bus crews, is bound to result in a better service to the travelling public; if costs rise too high, fares have to be increased and in some cases services have to be drastically reduced or abandoned.

A substantial proportion of the NBC companies stage carriage mileage is undertaken with one-man operated buses. This process of conversion has not been an easy process but within five or so years the conductor will probably be unknown except in very special circumstances.

If criticism can be levelled at bus company managements it is perhaps in the field of innovation and adaptability that they have been lacking. What teenager dressed for dancing wants to wait for a bus on a rainy windswept corner? Why not a bus shelter? The bus company answer is that it is the responsibility of the local authority to provide such facilities —and this is technically correct. But how many passengers have been lost by this lack of basic-amenity notwithstanding

174

the onus of provision? A perambulator can be placed in the guards compartment of a train, but what happens when the railway line is closed? There is no provision on buses for other than small collapsible push chairs but the young mother in the suburban or rural area is placed in great difficulty in travelling. Is it beyond the capabilities of engineers to design a bus with suitable entrance and drop ramp to cater for such traffic, the open part of the bus being used for standees in the peak period? The question of easier access to buses for the elderly and disabled has long been pressed and is now receiving attention by engineers on a national scale.

Territorial boundaries have in some instances led to problems of cross-boundary services leaving people without facilities they might have enjoyed if either major operator provided the complete network. The formation of the National Bus Company is gradually removing such boundary problems. Residents in municipal areas, although we would hasten to add not Exeter or Plymouth, have often been badly served due to parochial attitudes on the part of either the local authority bus undertaking or the company bus undertaking. As far as passengers are concerned a bus is a bus and it does not matter who operates it and what colour it is. Where joint agreements have resulted the benefits have accrued to to all concerned, bus operators, passengers and rate payers.

Another and perhaps surprising observation is that large bus undertakings have in some cases been too generous in their provision of rural facilities. The temptation in profitable days to add mileage to keep out a competitor has led to many a company being saddled with far too much unremunerative mileage.

There is also the concept of using buses for both passenger and goods transport, as is done extensively in Africa, Iceland and other regions of sparse population. In Britain, practically all bus companies undertake the conveyance of parcels up to a certain weight and this forms quite a significant proportion

175

of their revenue, particularly in the remoter districts. The main groups of articles conveyed are motor car spare parts, paint, newspapers, boxes of flowers and medical prescriptions and specimens; the latter is a very vital service and in some areas the general practitioner relies on the bus parcels service to maintain his link with the local hospitals. The old time country buses which took live animals, sides of bacon, churns of milk, boxes of fish, are alas things of the past but the conveyance of sundry goods is a side of their business which large bus companies could very well concentrate on building up, particularly as they are able to offer cheaper rates than the post office and usually deliver on the same day as despatch. With the boot on the other foot the post office itself has gone into the bus business with postal buses operating in remote areas, particularly in Scotland and Wales; one such service operates in the Honiton area of Devon.

Lastly there is the wider question of diversification of activities, which is in fact pursued by many local independent bus operators in Great Britain and by much larger operators in volatile countries such as Italy. This works largely on the principle of 'if you can't beat 'em, join 'em'; bus operators are in an excellent position to sell petrol to private cars, to carry out repairs on private cars, even to hire them out as a sideline and in Italy, the large Fiat car combine owns bus companies as a side activity. British bus operators have tended to say 'My business is carrying passengers, full stop'; history and evolution show that the organisation or animal which goes on following one idea or performing one function regardless, does indeed come to a full stop!

It is dangerous, but always tempting, to look into the future but one can hazard a guess that the future of road passenger transport lies in the urban areas and in inter-urban trunk routes. The progressive mechanisation of farming since 1945 resulting in the drift of working populations away from rural villages into towns and their replacement with a sophisticated middle class population who like to live in old cottages in the country and who inevitably own cars, gives little future hope for the traditional country bus service. On the other hand, the growing towns tend to place their new housing estates on the perimeter, so that the need for bus services from outlying town areas into the central shopping or industrial areas is growing. The increasing difficulty and cost of parking private cars in town centres will almost certainly lead ultimately to the establishment of perimeter car parks, with connecting bus services into town. This could lead to great improvements in free movement within town centres, as the bus services themselves are at present inhibited and impeded by general traffic congestion, although there is a growing tendency by local authorities to provide special bus lanes or to exempt buses from circuitous one way streets which apply to all other traffic. An initiative must also be taken by bus operators, to ensure that any new scheme gives rapid and efficient transport to and from town centres, so that the public as a whole are better off and not worse off, as a result of any restrictions which may be imposed on private transport. Convenient boarding points and stops placed to give maximum assistance to passengers will play a large part.

As far as concerns rural bus routes, it has been said many times that large operators should use mini-buses. The answer is that, if at no time during the course of its day's work the load carried does not exceed twelve people (a mini-bus), then a bus may not be justified economically at all. The size of a bus is determined by its peak hour loading and it would indeed be a false economy to put the big bus in the garage after the peak hour and bring out a substitute little bus—this would mean owning two units to do the work of one, with all the extra capital and maintenance costs involved. It would be equally uneconomical to duplicate the mini-bus at peak hours with a second or third mini-bus, since this would involve employing two or three drivers to do the work of one, and staff costs are by far the major item in a bus company's expenses. The small bus may well have a value in relation to the community bus schemes described elsewhere in this book but is not a justifiable economic proposition for maintaining regular stage services.

'Fares, please!' Bus services are not 'big business'—they exist on a multitude of small transactions, averaging 10p–15p which combine to produce the revenues of bus companies and the best method of collecting this money and of securing it against pilferage, has always taken up a large proportion of the bus manager's time. For many years, particularly between the two Wars, the usual practice was the employment of a separate conductor on each vehicle, who walked up and down collecting fares and issuing pre-priced tickets from a rack, which he clipped in the stage name or number at which the passenger boarded with a bell-punch giving a distinctive ring. Some small operators still employ this simple method but the large bus companies have replaced punches with ticket machines. Although the latter process began in the late 1930s, it gained momentum and was generally adopted between 1945 and 1955. Despite the greater capital cost of ticket machines, they enabled great savings to be made in clerical costs and eliminated the time consuming 'dead-end' jobs of making up conductors ticket boxes, checking and recording the opening and closing numbers of each denomination of tickets sold and reconciling them with cash handed in. Ticket machines in general print on a blank, tear-off strip, recording type of ticket (single, return, child, dog, parcel etc) ticket number, date of issue, stage number and amount of fare paid, the latter being recorded as a cumulative units figure by the machine. It is a simple matter, at the end of duty, to subtract opening from closing numbers registered by the machine and convert this to £p, to be checked against the cash handed in. Various statistical counters can be included on the machines to suit the needs of individual operators, eg number of tickets issued of a given denomination. Other types of machine have been used, some of which require the conductor to write the fare on the ticket, the amount being recorded on an audit strip in the machine; others used preprinted tickets in one form or another, the machine printing the value of the fare paid. The latest developments to assist in rapid fare-collection on busy one-man-operated routes, employ the most up-to-date electronic devices; the passenger inserts coins in the machine which, at the press of a button by the driver, dispenses a ticket. We are only at the beginning of a major revolution in fare-collection methods, which is growing in momentum, with the object of cutting costs and speeding up transactions.

Undoubtedly the motor-bus following in the wake of horse drawn stage coaches and wagonettes opened up the countryside and brought freedom of movement to communities which have remained virtually isolated for hundreds of years. Regular services were offered at reasonable fares and the standards of service and reliability achieved in the 1930s probably represented the industry at its best. Now the wheel has gone full circle; the countryside no longer needs opening up and has found its own means of travelling to and fro, and the transport industry must seek in the crowded and congested towns new means by which it can offer an attractive service to the community. The industry is not backward in advertising its wares, indeed a well-maintained bus is its own advertisement, but the National Bus Company has its own central publicity department in London, which designs everything from humorous or cryptic posters with a terse message to standardised lay-outs for timetable books and attractive leaflets suggesting places to be visited by bus, or walks in the countryside with the assistance of buses. Buses also obtain a small source of revenue from advertisements on side panels; they do not improve the appearance of the vehicle and can advertise their worst enemy, the private car!

Buses undoubtedly have a future; it never has been and never will be an easy one, as the industry deals in an intangible commodity (transport) which cannot be decked up, associated with sex or used to incite envy, to promote a quick sale. Also it deals essentially with people, their vagaries, their fluctuating requirements, their frustrating discontents, their occasional kindnesses; people are needed to run buses, to ride in them, to get in their way, to write rude words on them and about them, for everyone is a transport expert (except the bus manager, of course). No one would think of telling an accountant how to do his job, or a doctor, or an architect or even a boiler-maker or rodent operator—all these professions have their mystique—but the busman is everyone's fair target for criticism. The busman has to be a dedicated enthusiast, for his rewards are few and hard come by and his penalties are usually ulcers!

Appendix A

*Bristol Commercial Vehicles and Eastern
Coach Works - a brief history*

Bristol Commercial Vehicles

Only two major bus undertakings in Great Britain embarked on
the manufacture of their own buses, the Birmingham & Midland
Motor Omnibus Co Ltd and the Bristol Tramways & Carriage
Co Ltd. Since the purchase of the BET group by the National Bus
Company the BMMO (or to give the company its new name—
Midland Red) has given up its vehicle manufacturing activities
but the Bristol chassis, now under the control of a separate
company, Bristol Commercial Vehicles Ltd, has gone on from
strength to strength and now supplies chassis to both company
and municipal bus undertakings throughout Great Britain and
indeed some are exported to overseas operators.

The Bristol Tramways Co designed its first chassis, the C40 in
1908 and the first model (petrol engined, solid tyres, 4 ton) left
the works at Brislington later the same year; the body was also
built by the company. It was to be the forerunner of a long series
of types noteworthy for reliability and economical performance,
as a result of close liaison between the Company's construction
and operating departments. When the Tilling Organisation
obtained control of the Bristol Company in 1935, the Bristol
chassis was adopted generally by other Tilling subsidiaries. This
resulted in rapid development and expansion of the manufacturing side of the business, and a great number of G and J
chassis, mainly with Eastern Counties bodies, were built.
Although production almost ceased during World War II,
Bristol vehicles were soon on the home and overseas market
again after the end of hostilities. With the state ownership of the
Tilling Group under the Transport Act of 1947, a limitation was
placed on the number of Bristol chassis which could be built,
together with a stipulation that they could only be supplied to
companies in the nationalised Tilling group. It was not until 1955
that the manufacturing activities of the Bristol Company were

181

transferred to a separate organisation, Bristol Commercial Vehicles Ltd. The next important step took place in 1965, when agreement was reached between the Transport Holding Company and Leyland Motor Corporation for an exchange of share holdings, as a result of which Bristol chassis once again became available on the open market. Finally, with the establishment of the National Bus Company, a further change took place in September 1969, with the Leyland Truck & Bus Division acquiring a 50 per cent share holding in Bristol Commercial Vehicles, the National Bus Company holding the other 50 per cent. Day to day management of BCV now rests with the Leyland organisation.

As to the chassis themselves, in the early years they were used for both passenger and goods bodies and it is interesting to note that Bristol 4-tonners formed the backbone of the Devon Motor Transport fleet (see Chapter 2). Once again in the early 1950s a substantial number of goods vehicle chassis were produced for one customer—the Road Haulage Executive, the government agency managing the nationalised goods haulage fleet. The three most important milestones in chassis development have been the K and L type, the Lodekka and the RE. The K type double-decker (and corresponding L type single-decker) became the basic chassis for Tilling group fleets from 1938 until 1957 with of course intermediate improvements and alterations to the mechanical units and overall dimensions. The diesel engine used in this design included 4LW, 5LW and 6LW Gardner units, 6-cylinder AEC units and, from 1939 on, 6-cylinder Bristol AVW units, although the AVW did not go into general production until 1947 because of the war years. The Bristol Tramways & Carriage Co Ltd took delivery of the first K type bus, and Brighton, Hove & District purchased the last eight of this noble line.

The K and L type chassis were replaced by units of advanced design and particular mention must be made of the double deck Lodekka LD type. By utilising an off-set transmission with low level driving shafts, the centre gangway was lowered, enabling the step up from platform to lower deck to be abolished and more important, giving a centre gangway layout on the upper deck without exceeding the height of the previous 'lowbridge' type; this could only be achieved in previous vehicles by an inconvenient 'well' gangway at the side of the top deck. This design represented an important landmark in bus development; it was also built under licence by Dennis (the 'Lo-line' chassis) for non-Tilling companies. The single deck replacement for the L type was the LS chassis, with horizontal underfloor engine mounted amidships; this model was designed for integral construction, all bodies being manufactured by Eastern Coach Works. Production ceased in 1957 and the chassis was replaced by the MW model, a heavier unit designed for separate body construction.

The next major achievement in chassis development came in 1963 with the RE model, which had the engine located at the rear. Taking advantage of greater permitted lengths, the RE single decker has 53 seats and in effect can convey virtually the same number of passengers as the postwar double decker. Nevertheless, on many rural routes there was still a need for a smaller unit, accommodating fewer passengers and capable of negotiating country roads; to meet this demand the LH chassis was produced in 1967. This was a lightweight underfloor engine design, moderately priced and of a sturdy specification. It replaced various lightweight chassis developed in the late 1950s using proprietory units (the SC and SUS 30 seater and SUL 36 seater). Conversely both RE and LH have been built, in the case of the former to take 10 metre bodies and in the latter to take 11 metre bodies.

Returning to double deckers, the Lodekka was phased out of production in 1969 and replaced by the VR model (Vertical Rear engine), with the engine placed in the now popular transverse position across the rear of the chassis. The original prototype featured the engine longitudinally at the offside of the chassis; this interesting arrangement has not been widely produced but a batch was exported to South Africa and two batches have been built for Ribble Motor Services for use on Motorway Express coach services.

The Bristol chassis has always been popular in Great Britain, as a result of its sturdiness, reliability and economical performance, and the relaxation of the law in 1965 has enabled Bristol Commercial Vehicles to re-enter the commercial market with considerable success—a far cry from the original four tonner designed for internal use by the Bristol Tramways & Carriage Co Ltd. No account of the Company's activities would be complete without some amplification of their body building business. This dates back to the early days of the electric trams; work was commenced on a five acre site at Brislington in 1899 and the car building works came into operation the following year. The first job was to assemble the trucks and bodies for 150 tramcars to work the expanding electric car system. The following year the depot was the scene of 'a certain untoward incident'—in effect a strike. Strikes in 1901 were not the everyday thing that they are today and we find the company inserting the following advert in the Bristol *Mercury*:

> £100 REWARD. WHEREAS there is evidently an organised conspiracy on the part of certain DASTARDLY SCOUN-DRELS to injure the company utterly regardless of the lives and safety of the public of Bristol, and in order to encompass their vile purpose, they have maliciously designed and are still perpetuating a plan of placing obstructions such as IRON BOLTS AND RIVETS, PIECES OF ROD IRON, STONES etc. on the rails of the tramway . . .

After this turbulent start, the works settled down to producing some of the bodies for the Bristol company's diverse fleet of carriages, hearses and horse buses.

In 1906 the body for the Bristol company's first motor bus was made at Brislington, while in 1908 a start was made on motor taxicab bodies of which some 200 were built at the works. In 1910 a team of body makers was taken from Brislington and sent to work at Filton at the newly-formed aeroplane company, the latest offshoot of the Bristol company's management. Throughout 1912 and 1913, the bodyworks continued its diverse activities, constructing every form of road vehicle from char-a-bancs to brewers' lorries, but with the outbreak of World War I there was a complete change in 1915 to aircraft production. The first machines were the old 'box kites' followed by the Bristol Scout and later the Bristol Fighters—famous names in those war years.

Tramcar work was resumed in 1919 and, shortly after, the company embarked on a large programme of bus body building; the first were constructed at Filton aeroplane works but by 1925 Brislington was ready to commence manufacture of the HA type body. From then on, Bristol bodies were in continuous produc-tion, not only for the company's buses but for other companies and corporations throughout Britain. The first double deckers were built in 1926 for Manchester Corporation, while in 1930 the first lightweight all-metal bus was constructed. In 1938/9, as a result of the tramway replacement programme, no fewer than 200 bus bodies came out of the body building works.

World War II brought about a reversion to aircraft work, principally components for the Beaufighter, but in 1946 bus body work was resumed until 1954, when bus work was discontinued in favour of heavy goods vehicle cabs and platforms; thereafter Eastern Coachworks assumed responsibility for bus bodies.

Eastern Coach Works

Eastern Coach Works, Lowestoft, is the present body building counterpart of Bristol Commercial Vehicles. It originated in 1912 as part of United Automobile Services, which in the 1920s covered the whole of Eastern England from Suffolk to Yorkshire and Northumberland. When the Eastern Counties Omnibus Co Ltd was formed in 1931 to take over the United routes in East Anglia and certain other companies, the transfer included the body building business. Rapid expansion in the early 1930s and the production of bodies for associated Tilling companies, led in 1936 to the formation of a separate undertaking with the present title 'Eastern Coach Works Ltd'. The coach works was included in the transfer of the Tilling Group interests to the Tranport Holding Company and, like the Bristol chassis, its products were confined to the nationalised bus companies until 1965 when the exchange of shares with the Leyland Motor Corporation freed ECW bodies for the open market.

Eastern Coach Works is one of the leading bus and coach body builders in Great Britain; until 1946 hardwood and steel were principally employed but between 1946 and 1950 ECW pioneered the general use of aluminium alloy for bus bodywork and the use of this very durable but lightweight material has continued to the present day, supplemented now by reinforced glass fibre for complex shapes.

Although today the fleet of the Western National consists in the main of vehicles with Bristol chassis and ECW body, it also operates AEC, Leyland and Guy vehicles acquired with Devon General and Exeter City transport. These are progressively being replaced with ECW/Bristols but the latest deliveries have been Leyland National single deckers. Indeed a large number of vehicles of this type is already being operated by Plymouth City Transport.

Leyland National

The Leyland National is a direct result of the joint Leyland organisation and National Bus Company involvement referred to earlier in this appendix. In 1969 an agreement was reached between the NBC and the British Leyland Motor Corporation Ltd on the setting up of a jointly owned company—Leyland National Company Ltd in Cumberland for the production and marketing of a new single deck bus of integral construction. The new plant went into production in 1971 and the first new vehicles of the type were delivered in 1973.

The Leyland National bus is a whole new transport idea giving the operator a vehicle designed for his requirements, with an operating efficiency and reliability considerably in advance of other buses. It is specially designed for one-man operation and the driver has received a tremendous amount of attention. Controls are carefully laid out as dictated by ergonomic studies so that there is no waste of energy. For passengers, the Leyland National provides advanced comfort and safety and excellent riding qualities. Its performance by use of a turbocharged engine enables the bus to hold its own easily in all traffic conditions thereby benefiting other road users.

Over 40 are operated by Plymouth City Transport and others have entered service with Western National/Devon General.

Independent Operators

It is difficult to be specific as to the type of vehicles generally used by the smaller operators as all types are to be found in their fleets. If one is to generalise it would be on the basis that their school contract work is often performed with Bedford or Ford coaches, many of which have been purchased second-hand. At the other end of the range there are small operators who own some of the most modern coaches with bodies by Plaxton or Duple on Leyland, Volvo, or AEC chassis, together with the lighter Bedfords or Fords. Not all are on bus grants and there are independent operators of stage carriage services who also purchase new heavyweight vehicles of conventional stage carriage type. Again the workings can be intermixed and it is not unusual to see an expensive modern coach on a school contract if it is convenient to do this in conjunction with a private hire.

One problem in Devon is the need on both Dartmoor and Exmoor to operate vehicles over certain roads which are restricted to a maximum vehicle width of 7 ft 6 in. As such vehicles have to be specially built (with the exception of the Bedford SB) manufacturers are reluctant to produce small numbers with the result that it is usually the larger operators who purchase this type of vehicle new. This accounts to quite an extent for the demand for second-hand units of the narrow width variety.

Appendix B

List of Bus and Coach Businesses acquired by National Omnibus Transport Co Ltd and the Western and Southern National Omnibus Companies

1. Acquired by National

F. J. Arnold, Nailsworth, Stroud, Glos. (See chapter 2)	March 1920
Weymouth Motor Co Ltd, Edward St, Weymouth, Dorset (See chapter 2)	1925
Road Motors Ltd, Luton, Beds. (Branch at Weymouth)	April 1925
Isle of Portland Motor Bus Co Ltd, Portland, Dorset (See chapter 2)	1926
R. J. Smith (T/A Smith & Hoare), Portland, Dorset (See chapter 2)	1927
F. C. Hoare (T/A Smith & Hoare), Portland Dorset (See chapter 2)	1927
P. A. Court, Weymouth, Dorset	1927
Major H. Napier Rowlett, Rodborough Common, Stroud, Glos. (See chapter 2)	1927
Hardy Central Garage Co Ltd, Barnstaple (See chapter 2)	July 1927
Sam Edwards & Co, Flexbury Garage, Bude, Bude, Cornwall (See chapter 2)	1927
Devon Motor Transport Co Ltd, & Cornwall Motor Transport Co Ltd. (See chapter 2)	Nov 1927
J. Kershaw, North Petherton, Som. (See chapter 2)	1927
E. M. Jeanes (T/A Gem), Abbotsbury Rd, Weymouth, Dorset (See chapter 2)	1928
Trelawney Tours Ltd, Penzance, Cornwall (See chapter 2)	1928
G. R. Hocking (T/A Hockings Tours), Newquay, Cornwall (See chapter 2)	1928

Kirtcher & Dunham, Bridport, Dorset (See
    chapter 2)   1928
Butler Brothers (Bridport) Ltd, West St,
    Bridport, Dorset (See chapter 2)   1928

2. Western and Southern National Acquisitions

Bushell, Clovelly, Devon (See chapter 3)	1929
West Penwith Motor Co Ltd, St. Just, Cornwall (See chapter 3)	1929
J. G. Pullen (T/A Palace Saloons), Plymouth, Devon (See chapter 3)	May 1929
GWR Road Motor Department (See chapters 2 and 3)	1929
A. Braund, Braunton, Devon (See chapter 3)	1930
E. D. Hodges (T/A Hodges Motor Services), Combe Martin, Devon (See chapter 3)	1930
F. W. Squires, Barnstaple, Devon (See chapter 3)	
E. E. Piper, Devizes, Wilts (See chapter 3)	1931
Southern General Omnibus Co Ltd, Plymouth Devon (See chapter 3)	Nov 1931
Cornish Buses Ltd, Quay St, Truro, Cornwall (See chapter 3)	Nov 1931
Pennell & King, Crewkerne, Som	May 1932
Chaplin & Rogers, Chard, Som (See chapter 3)	June 1932
R. & M. Cox (T/A Wincanton Motor Services), N Cadbury, Som.	Nov 1932
J. C. Berryman, Townsend, Hayle, Cornwall (See chapter 3)	Nov 1932
E. E. Chalk, Torpoint, Cornwall	March 1933
Mrs E. E. Ellwood, Bradford Abbas, Sherborne, Dorset	March 1933
Edward Noyce & Son, Kingsbridge, Devon	March 1933
Albert H. Browning, Totnes, Devon	March 1933
Thomas Motors Ltd (T/A Lavender Blue), Taunton, Som (See chapter 3)	March 1933
E. V. Lowe & Co (T/A Zenith), Millbay Rd, Plymouth, Devon (See chapter 3)	March 1933
Browne Bros (T/A Zenith), Holbeton, Plymouth	April 1933
Mrs Williams, Plymouth, Devon	April 1933

P. G. Hanks, Bishops Lydeard, Som. (See
   chapter 3)   April 1933
H. V. Geen-Williams (T/A Imperial Service),
   Watchet, Som.   April 1933
Embankment Motor Co, Plymouth, Devon
   (Stage Services only acquired—See
   chapter 3)   1933
Edwards & Hann Ltd, Bridport, Dorset   April 1933
Mrs M Bassett, Knowle, Braunton, Devon   May 1933
A. H. Copp (T/A Royal Red), Ilfracombe,
   Devon   May 1933
Walden Brothers, Ilfracombe, Devon   May 1933
Courtney P. T. Hockin (T/A Hockin & Co),
   Sutcombe, Holsworthy, Devon   May 1933
Eli Ford (T/A Mascot Safety Coaches),
   Alcombe, Minehead, Som   May 1933
E. J. Dunn (T/A Dunn's Motor Service),
   Taunton Som (See chapter 3)   May 1933
A. Oxenham, Lynmouth, Devon   May 1933
Highways Ltd, 281 Regent St, London W1
   (See chapter 3)   May 1933
S. Lang, East-the-Water, Bideford   June 1933
B. C. Toogood (T/A Peter Pan), Shaftesbury,
   Dorset   Sept 1933
W. J. Ashton, Parkham, Bideford, Devon   Sept 1933
R. Ley, Parkham, Bideford, Devon   Sept 1933
Marazion Garage Ltd, Marazion, Penzance Oct 1933
Metford Day (T/A Stowey Favourite),
   Nether Stowey, Som   Oct 1933
R. Deacon (T/A Dorchester Motor Services),
   Dorchester, Dorset (See chapter 3)   Jan 1934
J. H. Pollard, Kuggar, Cornwall   Jan 1934
C. T. Ridgmont, Westonzoyland, Som.   Feb. 1934
C. J. Hobbs, Middlezoy, Som   March 1934
C. J. Way, W. Goodall & Lord (T/A
   Dartmouth & District Bus Co), Dartmouth,
   Devon (See chapter 3)   April 1934
E. Smith, Taunton, Som   May 1934
Elliott Brothers (Bournemouth) Ltd,
   (T/A Royal Blue) (See chapter 3)   Jan 1935
A. P. Oke, Bradworthy, Devon   Feb 1935

A. E. Taylor (T/A Sunbeam Coaches),	
Westbourne, Bournemouth, Hants.	Feb 1935
A. E. Good (T/A Silver Cars), Seaton, Devon	April 1935
A. T. Baker (T/A Pride of Lyme), Lyme Regis,	
Dorset (See chapter 3)	April 1935
Quay Garage Co Ltd, Kingsbridge, Devon	April 1935
W. V. Glanville (T/A Glanneys Cars),	
Bathpool, Taunton, Som	May 1935
Tourist Motor Coaches Ltd, 171 St Mary's	
Road, Southampton (See chaper 3)	May 1935
F. C. Hamlyn, Appledore, Devon	May 1935
Mrs E. M. Watson, Lyme Regis, Dorset	
(See chapter 3)	May 1935
A. L. Maddock, Week St Mary, Holsworthy,	
Devon	June 1935
J. Beer (T/A Bideford Motor Bus Co),	
Bideford, Devon	June 1935
Red Car Motor Co Ltd, Stithians, Cornwall	July 1935
A. E. Bath, Corscombe, Dorset	Aug 1935
W. H. Parker, Burton St David, Som	Aug 1935
Reynolds Bros, Padstow, Cornwall	
(See chapter 3)	Aug 1935
Dartington Hall Ltd, Dartington, Totnes,	
Devon	Nov 1935
Greyhounds Coaches (Weymouth) Ltd,	
Weymouth, Dorset	Dec 1935
Ernest A. B. Hocking (Hockings Ensign	
Carriages), Appledore, Devon	Jan 1936
T. H. Clapp, Seaton, Devon (See chapter 3)	Mar 1936
G. Brend, Bideford, Devon	Mar 1936
F. Sully & Sons (T/A Sully's Service), Chard,	
Som (See chapter 3)	April 1936
Scarlet Pimpernel Cars & Motor Supplies	
Ltd, Ilfracombe, Devon (See chapter 3)	March 1936
F. W. Dowell (T/A Orange & Black Coaching	
Services, Branscombe, Devon (See chapter 3)	Sept 1936
F. C. Hoare (T/A Portland Express),	
Portland, Dorset (See chapter 3)	Sept 1936
Webber, Boscastle	1936
R. J. Fancy (T/A Portland Express), Portland,	
Dorset (See chapter 3)	Sept 1936

L. A. S. Toleman (T/A Portland Express),
Portland, Dorset (See chapter 3) Sept 1936
C. R. Good & Son (T/A Pioneer), Beer, Devon
(See chapter 3) Sept 1936
Bird Bros (Transport) Ltd, Yeovil, Som March 1937
Bartlett & Nicholls (T/A Blue County Cars),
Langton Matravers, Dorset (See chapter 3) July 1937
G. Ford & Co (T/A The Safety Coaches),
Corfe Castle, Dorset July 1937
W. H. Miles & S. G. Lee (Coombe Bus),
Coombe St Nicholas, Chard, Som
(See chapter 3) July 1937
W. H. Charles, Leigh, Sherborne, Dorset July 1937
S. Pulford (T/A Wivey Coaches), Langley,
Wiveliscombe, Som July 1937
Mrs E. M. Jeanes (T/A Gem), Westham,
Weymouth, Dorset (Tours—Stage Services
sold to National in 1928) Oct 1937
C. F. S. Gillham (T/A Blue Bird), Bridport,
Dorset May 1938
Frederick R. Simpson & Sons, Woolacombe,
Devon May 1938
S. T. Hard & Son (T/A Red Deer Coaches),
Timberscombe, Som (See chapter 3) May 1938
Riders Garages Ltd, Falmouth, Cornwall June 1938
Truscott Bros, Rilla Mill, Callington, Cornwall
(See chapter 3) July 1938
J. H. Venner, N. Petherwin, Launceston,
Cornwall July 1938
T. Edwards, W. C. Mann, H. Spry &
J. W. Hallett, Bude, Cornwall (Tours—
Stage Services sold to National in 1927)
(See chapter 3) March 1939
H. & P. Rosewarne (T/A Mayqueen Service),
Porthleven, Cornwall May 1939
A. Richards (T/A City of Truro), Truro,
Cornwall 1939
T. W. Billinghurst, Saltash, Cornwall
(See chapter 3) Aug 1939
J. G. Mitchell, Creech St Michael, Taunton,
Som (See chapter 3) 1945

Foxworthy (T/A Dart Bus Service), Stoke
    Gabriel, Devon (See chapter 3)   Feb 1952
Quantock Hauliers Ltd, Watchet, Som
    (See chapter 3)   Feb 1952
Blakes Bus Services Ltd, Delabole, Cornwall
    (See chapter 3)   1952
Prout, Port Isaac, Cornwall (See chapter 3)   1953
Porlock Weir, Porlock & Minehead Motor
    Services Ltd (T/A Portlock Blue Motors)
    (See chapter 3)   1953
Banfill & Barrington (T/A Selene Coaches),
    Mawnan Smith, Cornwall (See chapter 3)   1953
Heybrook Bay Motor Services Ltd, Down
    Thomas, Devon (See chapter 3)   1959
Lewis Motors (Falmouth) Ltd, Falmouth,
    Cornwall (See chapter 3)   1965
J. M. Hitchens & Sons, Newlyn, Cornwall
    (See chapter 3)   1966
Millbrook Steamboat & Trading Co Ltd   1968
Greenslades Tours Ltd (tours from
    Sidmouth)   1977
A. J. & M. D. Lovering, Combe Martin
    (Stage services only)   1978

Appendix C

Operators acquired by the Devon General Omnibus and Touring Co Ltd

Croscols	1924	Tiverton—Dulverton Tiverton—Exeter Tiverton—Cullompton —Uffculme
Fleet Cars Ltd, Torquay	1924	Tours
Comfy Coaches, Paignton	1925	Tours
White Heather Tours, Paignton	1925	Tours
E. O. Babington, Ashburton	1926	Ashburton—Torquay
Torquay and Chelston Steam Car Co Ltd	1927	Torquay—Plymouth
J. Mills (Bluebird), Brixham	1931	Paignton—Brixham
Prout, Churston	1931	Paignton—Brixham
J. Low, Paignton	1931	Paignton—Brixham
H. Cooper (Dandy Cars), Paignton	1931	Paignton—Brixham
Soul & Sanders (Paigntonian) Paignton	1931	Paignton—Brixham
J. Geddes (Burton Cars), Brixham	1931	Paignton—Brixham service only
Grey Cars (Torquay subsidiary of A. Timpson & Sons Ltd, Catford, London)	1932	Tours
R. P. Summers, Ottery St Mary	1934	Ottery St Mary—Exeter
Sidmouth Motor Co and Dagworthy Ltd.	1934	Sidmouth—Exeter and Sidmouth—Sidbury

(Note: this company retained its Tours and local stage services at Sidmouth until 1956—see below)

A. C. Aggett, Marldon	1935	Paignton—Marldon
Milton Bus Service, Crediton	1935	Exeter—Crediton and Crediton local services
Teignmouth Motor Car Co	1936	Teignmouth local services

Miller & Son, Exmouth	1938	Exmouth local services
W. J. Abbott Ltd, Exmouth	1940	Exmouth local services
The Witheridge and Tiverton area stage services of Greenslades Tours, subsequently shared with Southern National under a territorial agreement	1948	
Hart, Budleigh Salterton	1952	Exmouth—Budleigh Salterton—Ladram Bay
Balls Ltd, Newton Abbot	1952	Newton Abbot—Maidencombe and Shaldon
A. E. Townsend, Torquay	1952	Tours from Torquay
H. D. Gourd and Sons, Bishopsteignton	1955	Bishopsteignton—Teignmouth and Newton Abbot
The remaining portion of the business of Sidmouth Motor Co and Dagworthy Ltd, the tours going to Greenslades Tours Ltd, and the Sidmouth—Peak Hill and Salcombe Regis stage services to Devon General	1956	
Falkland Garages Ltd, Torquay	1957	Tours from Torquay
Court Garages (Torquay) Ltd and its associated car hire firm of Bute Court Garages Ltd	1966	
Greenslades Tours Ltd	1978	Tours from Torbay

Appendix D

Railway Lines and Stations in the area closed to passenger traffic since 1945

1948 Clyst St Mary & Digby Halt
1949 Nailsworth—Stonehouse
1951 Burnham-on-Sea—Highbridge
      Faringdon—Uffington
      Malmesbury—Little Somerford
      Plymouth—Turnchapel
      Glastonbury—Wells
1952 Weymouth—Portland—Easton
      Weymouth—Abbotsbury
1953 Swindon—Highworth
      Bristol (St Philips)—Fishponds
1955 Local stations between Warminster and Salisbury
      Beanacre Halt
1956 Yelverton—Princetown
1957 Probus—Ladock Platform
1958 Teign Valley Line: Exeter—Heathfield
      Totnes—Ashburton
1959 Newton Abbot—Mortonhampstead
      Barnstaple (Victoria Road Stn.)
      Local stations between Plymouth and Brent
      Gloucester—Ledbury
      Bristol—Frome
1960 Carn Brea Station
      Local stations between Cheltenham & Honeybourne
1961 Local stations between Bristol and Swindon
      Cheltenham—Swindon—Severnake—Andover
      Norton Fitzwarren Station
1962 Local stations between Langport and Castle Cary
      Launceston—Plymouth
      Taunton—Chard Junction
      Gwinear Road—Helston
      Dursley—Coaley
      Cheltenham—Kingham
      Sutton Bingham Halt
1963 Brent—Kingsbridge
      Culm Valley Line: Tiverton Junc—Hemyock
      Exe Valley Line: Exeter—Dulverton
      Chacewater—Newquay
      Churston—Brixham
      Yatton—Cheddar—Wells—Witham Friary
1964 Knowle Halt
      Local stations between Swindon and Didcot
      Tiverton Junction—Tiverton
      Local stations between Exeter and Taunton
      Local stations between Plymouth and Penzance
      Local stations between Bristol and Taunton
      Brent Station
      Langport—Yeovil
      Local stations between Taunton and Langport

	Kemble—Cirencester		Seaton Junction—Seaton
	Kemble—Tetbury		Local stations between Bath
	Bristol—Portishead		and Weymouth
	Bristol—New Passage—		Okehampton—Bude
	Severn Beach		Halwill Juntion—
	Berkley Road—Lydney		Wadebridge
	Gloucester—Hereford		Yatton—Clevedon
	Local stations between		Northam Station
	Swindon and Gloucester		Local stations between
1965	Lostwithiel—Fowey		Trowbridge and
	Local stations between		Chippenham
	Bristol and Gloucester		Local stations between
	Torrington—		Westbury and Bedwyn
	Halwill Junction		Cheltenham Spa (Malvern
	Chippenham—Calne		Road and St James
	Axminster—Lyme Regis		Stations)
	Local stations between	1967	Sidmouth Junction—
	Bristol and Swindon via Bath		Sidmouth
	Local stations between		Tipton St John—Exmouth
	Gloucester and Worcester		Bodmin Road—Padstow
	Yeovil Town—Yeovil, Pen	1968	Yeovil Junction—
	Mill		Yeovil Turn
1966	Taunton—Barnstaple		Okehampton—Bere Alston
	Barnstaple—Torrington	1969	Badminton Station
	Local stations between	1970	Barnstaple—Ilfracombe
	Exeter and Salisbury		St Annes Park and Saltford
	Somerset &Dorset Line:		Stations
	Bournemouth—Bath,	1971	Taunton—Minehead
	Highbridge and Bristol		Brent Knoll Station
	Patney & Chirton—	1972	Wareham—Swanage
	Holt Junction		Exeter—Okehampton
	Callington—Gunnislake		

Index